P9-AFA-873

UNM-GALLUP   DUP

3 7996 1006 8085 5

Psychological
Disorders

Alzheimer's Disease and Other Dementias

Psychological Disorders

Psychological Disorders

Alzheimer's Disease and Other Dementias

Sonja M. Lillrank, M.D., Ph.D.

Consulting Editor
Christine Collins, Ph.D.
Research Assistant
Professor of Psychology
Vanderbilt University

Foreword by
Pat Levitt, Ph.D.
Vanderbilt Kennedy
Center for Research
on Human Development

CHELSEA HOUSE
PUBLISHERS
An imprint of Infobase Publishing

Psychological Disorders: Alzheimer's Disease and Other Dementias

Copyright © 2007 by Infobase Publishing

All rights reserved. No part of this book may be reproduced or utilized in any form or by any means, electronic or mechanical, including photocopying, recording, or by any information storage or retrieval systems, without permission in writing from the publisher. For information contact:

Chelsea House
An imprint of Infobase Publishing
132 West 31st Street
New York NY 10001

ISBN-10: 0-7910-9005-1
ISBN-13: 978-0-7910-9005-3

Library of Congress Cataloging-in-Publication Data

Lillrank, Sonja. M.
  Psychological disorders : Alzheimer's disease and other dementias / Sonja. M. Lillrank ; foreword by Pat Levitt.
      p. cm.
  Includes bibliographical references and index.
  ISBN 0-7910-9005-1 (hc : alk. paper)
  1. Dementia—Juvenile literature. I. Title
  RC521.L55 2007
  616.8'3—dc22   2006010414

Chelsea House books are available at special discounts when purchased in bulk quantities for businesses, associations, institutions, or sales promotions. Please call our Special Sales Department in New York at (212) 967-8800 or (800) 322-8755.

You can find Chelsea House on the World Wide Web at http://www.chelseahouse.com

Text and cover design by Keith Trego

Printed in the United States of America

Bang EJB 10 9 8 7 6 5 4 3 2

This book is printed on acid-free paper.

All links and Web addresses were checked and verified to be correct at the time of publication. Because of the dynamic nature of the Web, some addresses and links may have changed since publication and may no longer be valid.

Table of Contents

Foreword

Pat Levitt, Ph.D.
Vanderbilt Kennedy
Center for Research
on Human Development

Think of the most complicated aspect of our universe, and then multiply that by infinity! Even the most enthusiastic of mathematicians and physicists acknowledge that the brain is by far the most challenging entity to understand. By design, the human brain is made up of billions of cells called neurons, which use chemical neurotransmitters to communicate with each other through connections called synapses. Each brain cell has about 2,000 synapses. Connections between neurons are not formed in a random fashion, but rather, are organized into a type of architecture that is far more complex than any of today's supercomputers. And, not only is the brain's connective architecture more complex than any computer, its connections are capable of *changing* to improve the way a circuit functions. For example, the way we learn new information involves changes in circuits that actually improve performance. Yet some change can also result in a disruption of connections, like changes that occur in disorders such as drug addiction, depression, schizophrenia, and epilepsy, or even changes that can increase a person's risk of suicide.

Genes and the environment are powerful forces in building the brain during development and ensuring normal brain functioning, but they can also be the root causes of psychological and neurological disorders when things go awry. The way in which brain architecture is built before birth and in childhood will determine how well the brain functions when we are adults, and even how susceptible we are to such diseases as depression, anxiety, or attention disorders, which can severely disturb brain function. In a sense, then, understanding how the brain is built can lead us to a clearer picture of the ways in which our brain works, how we can improve its functioning, and what we can do to repair it when diseases strike.

Brain architecture reflects the highly specialized jobs that are performed by human beings, such as seeing, hearing, feeling, smelling, and moving. Different brain areas are specialized to control specific functions. Each specialized area must communicate well with other areas for the brain to accomplish even more complex tasks, like controlling body physiology—our patterns of sleep, for example, or even our eating habits, both of which can become disrupted if brain development or function is disturbed in some way. The brain controls our feelings, fears, and emotions; our ability to learn and store new information; and how well we recall old information. The brain does all this, and more, by building, during development, the circuits that control these functions, much like a hard-wired computer. Even small abnormalities that occur during early brain development through gene mutations, viral infection, or fetal exposure to alcohol can increase the risk of developing a wide range of psychological disorders later in life.

Those who study the relationship between brain architecture and function, and the diseases that affect this bond, are neuroscientists. Those who study and treat the disorders that are caused by changes in brain architecture and chemistry are psychiatrists and psychologists. Over the last 50 years, we have learned quite a lot about how brain architecture and chemistry work and how genetics contribute to brain structure and function. Genes are very important in controlling the initial phases of building the brain. In fact, almost every gene in the human genome is needed to build the brain. This process of brain development actually starts prior to birth, with almost all the neurons we will ever have in our brain produced by mid-gestation. The assembly of the architecture, in the form of intricate circuits, begins by this time, and by birth, we have the basic organization laid out. But the work is not yet complete, because billions of connections form over a remarkably long period of time, extending through puberty. The brain of a child is being built and modified on a daily basis, even during sleep.

While there are thousands of chemical building blocks, such as proteins, lipids, and carbohydrates, that are used, much like bricks and mortar, to put the architecture together, the highly detailed connectivity that emerges during childhood depends greatly upon experiences and our environment. In building a house, we use specific blueprints to assemble the basic structures, like a foundation, walls, floors, and ceilings. The brain is assembled similarly. Plumbing and electricity, like the basic circuitry of the brain, are put in place early in the building process. But for all of this early work, there is another very important phase of development, which is termed experience-dependent development. During the first three years of life, our brains actually form far more connections than we will ever need, almost 40 percent more! Why would this occur? Well, in fact, the early circuits form in this way so that we can use experience to mold our brain architecture to best suit the functions that we are likely to need for the rest of our lives.

Experience is not just important for the circuits that control our senses. A young child who experiences toxic stress, like physical abuse, will have his or her brain architecture changed in regions that will result in poorer control of emotions and feelings as an adult. Experience is powerful. When we repeatedly practice on the piano or shoot a basketball hundreds of times daily, we are using experience to model our brain connections to function at their finest. Some will achieve better results than others, perhaps because the initial phases of circuit-building provided a better base, just like the architecture of houses may differ in terms of their functionality. We are working to understand the brain structure and function that result from the powerful combination of genes building the initial architecture and a child's experience adding the all-important detailed touches. We also know that, like an old home, the architecture can break down. The aging process can be particularly hard on the ability of brain circuits to function at their best because positive change comes less readily as we get older. Synapses may be lost and brain chemistry can change over time. The difficulties in understanding how architecture gets built are paralleled by the complexities of what happens to that architecture as we grow older. Dementia associated with brain deterioration as a complication of Alzheimer's disease, or memory loss associated with aging or alcoholism are active avenues of research in the neuroscience community.

There is truth, both for development and in aging, in the old adage "use it or lose it." Neuroscientists are pursuing the idea that brain architecture and chemistry can be modified well beyond childhood. If we understand the mechanisms that make it easy for a young, healthy brain to learn or repair itself following an accident, perhaps we can use those same tools to optimize the functioning of aging brains. We already know many ways in which we can improve the functioning of the aging or injured brain. For example, for an individual who has suffered a stroke that has caused structural damage to brain architecture, physical exercise can be quite powerful in helping to reorganize circuits so that they function better, even in an elderly individual. And you know that when you exercise and sleep regularly, you just feel better. Your brain chemistry and architecture are functioning at their best. Another example of ways we can improve nervous system function are the drugs that are used to treat mental illnesses. These drugs are designed to change brain chemistry so that the neurotransmitters used for communication between brain cells can function more normally. These same types of drugs, however, when taken in excess or abused, can actually damage brain chemistry and change brain architecture so that it functions more poorly.

As you read the series Psychological Disorders, the images of altered brain organization and chemistry will come to mind in thinking about complex diseases such as schizophrenia or drug addiction. There is nothing more fascinating and important to understand for the well-being of humans. But also keep in mind that as neuroscientists, we are on a mission to comprehend human nature, the way we perceive the world, how we recognize color, why we smile when thinking about the Thanksgiving turkey, the emotion of experiencing our first kiss, or how we can remember the winner of the 1953 World Series. If you are interested in people, and the world in which we live, you are a neuroscientist, too.

Pat Levitt, Ph.D.
Director, Vanderbilt Kennedy Center
for Research on Human Development
Vanderbilt University
Nashville, Tennessee

What Is Dementia?

THE CASE OF A HIGH-SCHOOL TEACHER

George was a 61-year-old high-school science department head
who was an experienced and enthusiastic camper and hiker. One
day while hiking in the woods he suddenly and unexpectedly
became extremely fearful and barely made it back to his car before
dark. Over the next few months, he slowly started losing interest
in his usual hobbies. For example, he used to love reading, but
suddenly lost interest in books, and he never hiked again. He
started having problems keeping his checkbook balanced, problems with simple calculations. On several occasions he became lost
while driving in areas that used to be familiar to him. Since he
was aware that something was not right with his memory, he
began to write notes to himself so that he would not forget to do
errands. In an unusual change for him, he abruptly decided to
retire from work, without discussing it with anyone beforehand.
After he retired, he spent most of the day sorting small things in
the house and then transporting them to another spot in the
house. He became stubborn and argued easily. After a while he
needed help in shaving and dressing.

Six years after the first symptoms had developed, he had a
physical exam. He couldn't tell the doctor where he was or what
the date and day of the week were. He could not remember the
names of his college and graduate school or the subject in which
he majored. He could describe his job by title only. In 1978 he

thought John F. Kennedy was president of the United States. His speech was fluent and clear, but he had difficulty finding words. He used many long, meaningless phrases as if to give the impression that he could keep a social conversation. He called a cup a vase, and identified the rims of glasses as "the holders." He could not do simple calculations. He could not copy a picture of a cube or draw a house. He had no idea that there was something wrong with him.

A physical exam revealed nothing abnormal, and routine laboratory tests were also normal. A computed tomography scan of his brain showed that his brain had shrunk. His condition deteriorated, and he required admission to a general hospital within a year of this physical exam. Over the next year he stopped speaking. He would pace back and forth constantly on the ward. Once he escaped from a locked ward and was found wandering aimlessly some miles from the hospital. Physically he looked like there was nothing wrong with him, whereas his decline intellectually was obvious. Eventually he began to lose weight, took to bed, and developed contractures (permanent muscular contractions). He died at age 72 of pneumonia. An exam of his brain after his death confirmed the diagnosis of Alzheimer's disease.[1]

DEFINITION OF DEMENTIA

Dementias are brain disorders that impair memory, thinking, and behavior. The word *dementia* comes from Latin and means "away" and "mind." Dementia is a clinical syndrome, or condition, that presents several different symptoms of which memory problems and impaired intellectual functioning are the hallmark. Dementia is not one specific disease. Instead, dementia is a descriptive term for a collection of symptoms that can be caused by a number of different diseases or traumas that affect the brain. Dementia is often difficult to diagnose. In most cases the first signs of dementia are mild, then these signs worsen at a steady pace. For known and unknown reasons, irreversible

Figure 1.1 A researcher tests an elderly man for signs of Alzheimer's disease. In this timed test, the man must fit geometric, wooden shapes into the corresponding template. © *Southern Illinois University/Photo Researchers, Inc.*

changes occur in the brain's nerve cells (**neurons**). The damage to the neurons is often progressive and can gradually lead to the destruction of the neurons. Improperly functioning neurons cause communication problems in and between different brain regions that are vital for normal brain functioning. Dementias generally affect people over the age of 65, but some types of dementia can also affect teenagers and adults. Currently, there is no cure for dementia, and it ultimately leads to death.

Besides a gradual loss of memory, other common symptoms of dementias include difficulty learning, loss of language skills, disorientation, and problems with reasoning and judgment. As a result of memory impairment, patients often forget how to use certain objects. For example, they may forget how to use a comb, a toothbrush, or eat with utensils. A painful symptom for the family is that patients may not recognize their loved ones. Patients may also get lost, even in familiar surroundings, and may repeat the same story over and over again. In later stages, they may have trouble finding words and may not be able to make responsible decisions. As the condition progresses, people often go through changes in their personalities. Patients with more advanced dementia need more and more help to function in normal life and to stay safe. They may need help in all aspects of life, including bathing, eating, using the restroom, and getting dressed. They also may develop behavioral problems like agitation, anxiety, wandering, **delusions** (fixed false beliefs) and **hallucinations** (seeing, hearing, or feeling things that do not exist). An example of a delusion would be when someone wrongly believes that family members are trying to poison him or steal his valuables. Some of these symptoms can be helped with medications.

It is important to remember that the symptoms of dementia can vary a lot in different people and with different types of dementia. In some kinds of dementia, patients may develop **neurological** problems at the end stage of the disease. A neurological problem involves difficulty maintaining balance and walking. These problems happen when the deterioration of the

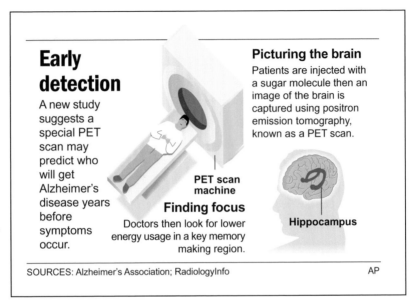

Figure 1.2 Graphic shows how a PET scan could illuminate early signs of Alzheimer's disease © *AP Images*

brain affects areas that are involved in coordination and movement. Patients with severe dementia often become bedridden and need to be hospitalized.

There are several different types of dementias and different diseases that cause dementia. Dementias include Alzheimer's dementia, vascular dementia (VaD), Parkinson's dementia, dementia with Lewy bodies, Pick's disease, or other frontotemporal dementias, and Huntington's disease. Infections that affect the brain like human immunodeficiency virus (HIV) and Creutzfeldt-Jakob disease (CJD), as well as head trauma, can also lead to dementia. Even though we do not yet have a cure for dementias, early diagnosis is important. The progress of some kinds of dementia can be halted or slowed if the problem is detected early, and treatment of the first symptoms may allow the patient to be cared for at home for a longer time before hospitalization becomes necessary. Early treatment can have a great effect on the quality of life of patients and their caregivers.

In the chapters that follow we will explore some of the symptoms of different dementias, causes, treatment, and ongoing research, and look at what you can do to help someone who is suffering from dementia.

Statistical and Epidemiological Facts

The greatest risk factor for developing most dementias is increasing age. In affluent countries, eliminating many diseases, reducing infant mortality, and improving standards of living have all increased life expectancy. Over the past 30 years, there has been a 60-percent decline in mortality from **cerebrovascular disease** (narrowing of the blood vessels in the brain) and a 30-percent decline in mortality from coronary artery disease. In the United States life expectancy has increased with every decade. In 1900 life expectancy was 48 years, while in 1995 it was 75.8 years. Longer life spans have led to a dramatic increase in the number of elderly people who live past the age of 100. In 1900 4.1 percent of the U.S. population was 65 or older; in 1995 the number increased to 12.8 percent; it is predicted to be 20 percent by the year 2050.[2] That means that more than 34 million people today are 65 or older. The number of people over age 65 will continue to increase rapidly as the "baby boom" generation (people born in the years after World War II) reaches age 65.

The number of older people is increasing, and so is the number of people who suffer from dementias. Of people in the United States older than age 65, approximately 15 percent have mild dementia and 5 percent have severe dementia. Of people older than 80, roughly 20 percent have severe dementia.[3]

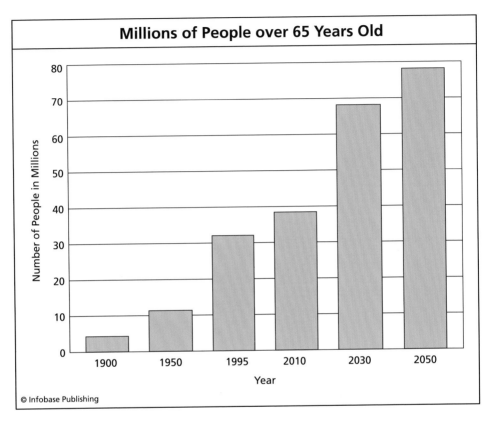

Figure 1.3 The number of people age 65 or older in the United States rose steadily during the 20th century and is projected to continue rising for several decades.

Facts About Alzheimer's Dementia

The most common type of dementia is Alzheimer's disease, accounting for approximately 50 to 60 percent of all patients with dementia. An estimated 4.5 million Americans have Alzheimer's disease.[4] Increasing age is the greatest risk factor for Alzheimer's dementia. The number of Americans who have Alzheimer's disease will continue to grow as the population gets older. It has been estimated that by the year 2050 the

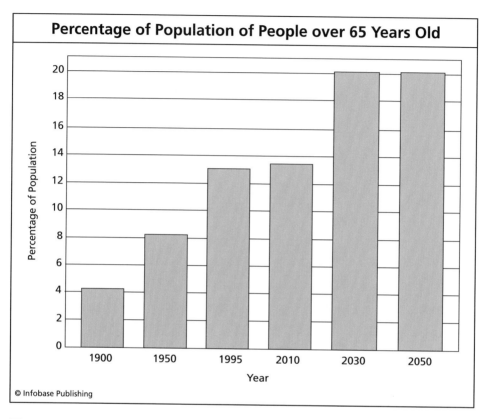

Figure 1.4 Growth is expected in other segments of the population, but the percentage of people age 65 or older is expected to continue growing.

number of people with Alzheimer's could range from 11.3 million to 16 million.

It has been estimated that Alzheimer's disease affects one in 10 individuals over age 65 and nearly half of those over 85.[5] It is the fourth leading cause of death among adults, and approximately 100,000 people die each year as a result of complications from Alzheimer's disease. However, most people with Alzheimer's die of other causes, and the dementia is not reflected on death certificates or in official statistics.[6] Patients with dementia of the Alzheimer's type occupy 50 percent of

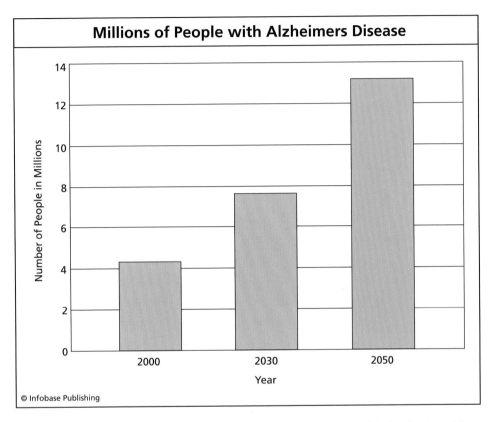

Millions of People with Alzheimers Disease

© Infobase Publishing

Figure 1.5 Alzheimer's disease is most common among the elderly. As the elderly population continues to rise, the number of Alzheimer's cases is expected to grow with it.

nursing home beds, which significantly adds to the cost of the disorder.[3]

Alzheimer's disease affects more women than men because women tend to live longer than men.[7] Studies have also shown that Alzheimer's disease is more common among the Latino and African-American populations as compared with white populations. The reason for this is not clear but environmental factors have been suggested. A study published in 2004 by researchers at the Memory Disorders Clinic at the University of Pennsylvania showed that Latino subjects developed

Alzheimer's disease on average almost seven years earlier than the non-Latino group.[8] Studies have shown that although black populations in Africa and the United States have the same genetic risk factors for Alzheimer's dementia, it is more likely for African Americans to develop the disease.[7]

Alzheimer's Disease Can Affect Anyone

Ronald Wilson Reagan, the 40th president of United States, revealed in 1994, when he was 83, that he was suffering from Alzheimer's disease. As president in 1983, he approved the creation of a task force to coordinate and oversee research on Alzheimer's disease. That same year, the U.S. Congress declared November "National Alzheimer's Disease Month." President Reagan's open disclosure of his illness dramatically reduced the stigma associated with this deadly degenerative disease. Together with his wife, Nancy, he launched the Nancy and Ronald Reagan Research Institute at the Alzheimer's Association in 1995 and helped raise millions of dollars for research. Reagan died in 2004 from complications of the disease. Nancy Reagan has continued his work as a forceful advocate for the sake of those who suffer from this devastating disease.

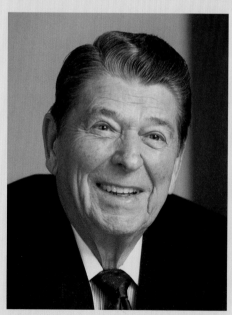

Figure 1.6 President Ronald Reagan. © *AP Images*

VASCULAR DEMENTIA

The second most common type of dementia is vascular dementia, which is related to cerebrovascular and cardiovascular diseases. In cerebrovascular disease, the blood vessels that supply the brain with oxygen and nutrients get narrower, and in cardiovascular disease, also called **ischemic heart disease**, the blood vessels that supply the heart muscle with oxygen and nutrients narrow. These diseases can cause **strokes** and heart disease (heart attacks) in the elderly. The most common causes of illness and deaths in the elderly are stroke and ischemic heart disease.[9] In a stroke, a blood clot blocks a blood vessel in the brain, permanently damaging its ability to supply oxygen and nutrients to cells in that area. In ischemic heart disease, the heart cannot pump enough blood to function because of damaged blood vessels in the heart muscle and, as a result, the brain does not get enough nutrients and oxygen. In a heart attack, a blood clot blocks a blood vessel in the heart, causing damage to parts of the heart muscle and leading similarly to less effective blood supply to the brain.

Vascular dementia accounts for about 15 to 30 percent of all dementias and is most common in people between the ages of 60 and 70. Vascular dementia is more common among men, especially in those who suffer from hypertension (high blood pressure) or other cardiovascular risk factors like high cholesterol or diabetes. Since this type of dementia has an underlying cause, it is important to prevent or treat the illness that can increase the possibility of vascular dementia.

Interestingly, vascular dementia has historically been common in Russia and Japan, whereas Alzheimer's disease is more common in North America, Scandinavia, and Europe.[10] Japan, however, has had increased life expectancy and better management of stroke risk factors like high blood pressure, and as a result Alzheimer's has become the most common type of dementia.[7]

OTHER DEMENTIAS

Other kinds of dementia each represent about one to five per-cent of all cases. These include Parkinson's dementia, fron-totemporal dementia, Huntington's disease, alcohol-induced dementia, and head trauma. Dementia can also be caused by infections to the brain and hereditary diseases like Wilson's dis-ease. Huntington's disease is an involuntary movement disor-der that is often associated with dementia. Parkinson's disease is a progressive brain disorder and a movement disorder that is also commonly associated with dementia. Approximately 20 to 30 percent of patients with Parkinson's disease have dementia.

Alcohol dependency is the most common cause of drug-induced dementias. A person who is dependent on alcohol or an illicit drug is using these substances every day in large amounts and usually develops tolerance to the drug, which means that he needs more of the drug to get the same effect as before. The per-son is in danger of getting dangerous withdrawal symptoms if he stops the drug abruptly. He or she usually is not able to keep a job or support a family because much of his or her time goes to finding and using the drug he is dependent on. Dependency on drugs such as inhalants, sedatives, hypnotics, and **anxiolytics** (also called benzodiazepines) can also cause dementia. These drugs can all cause direct damage to the brain. Prevention of any drug abuse that often leads to dependency could reduce the number of these dementias, which often affect people younger than 65 years old.[3]

DEMENTIA IN YOUNGER PEOPLE

In people between the ages of 21 and 65, the most common causes of dementia are acquired immunodeficiency syndrome (AIDS), drug and alcohol abuse, head trauma, and multiple sclerosis and other **demyelinating diseases**. Head trauma and

infections such as AIDS can cause dementia at any age by causing direct damage to the brain. These will be discussed in more
detail in Chapter 4.

Common causes of dementia in adolescents are metabolic
abnormalities like Wilson's disease and drug and alcohol abuse,
specifically overdose. A metabolic disease is a disease that is
generally diagnosed in early childhood because the growing
person fails to thrive. In Wilson's disease, the body cannot get
rid of excess copper, which then accumulates in the brain and
various other organs, causing dementia and involuntary movements. Wilson's disease is quite rare, affecting about 1 out of
100,000 people. [11]

Demyelinating diseases like multiple sclerosis sometimes
cause dementia as a symptom. In a demyelinating disease, the
"**myelin sheaths**" that cover **axons** of neurons get inflamed and
are then stripped of myelin, or are demyelinated.[12] This kind of
damage to the neuron makes it difficult or even impossible for
the neuron to do its usual job: transferring information from
one end of the neuron to the other as electric impulses. This
then leads to various neurological problems including muscle
weakness, tingling feelings, vision problems, etc.

Degenerative diseases like Huntington's disease or other rare,
usually genetically transmitted diseases may also cause dementia in adolescents. This illness destroys neurons in a specific
brain area called caudate nuclei. It causes involuntary movements like brief, jerky, brisk, purposeless movements in the
limbs, face and trunk that look like a random "dance."

DEMENTIA AFFECTS THE FAMILY AND FINANCES

Dementias have a big impact on family life, especially if the
patient is being cared for at home. A person with Alzheimer's
disease will live an average of eight years but as many as 20
years or more from the onset of symptoms.[6] Families with

members who suffer from Alzheimer's disease or other dementias are affected emotionally, financially, and physically by the burden of caring for the loved one who has dementia. It is extremely stressful to care for someone who constantly forgets who the caregiver is or cannot recognize family members. It can be emotionally very draining when the patient has hostile, aggressive outbursts, is disoriented, and needs supervision for his or her own safety both day and night. Caregivers of patients with Alzheimer's disease have been shown to be at risk for developing depression.[13]

Families are also affected financially. The National Institute of Aging and the Alzheimer's Association have estimated that the direct and indirect costs of caring for individuals with Alzheimer's disease in the United States are at least $100 billion per year.[14, 15] It has been estimated that about seven out of 10 people with Alzheimer's disease live at home. Family and friends provide almost 75 percent of the care at home.[6] The remainder is paid care that costs an average of $12,500 a year, based on a 1993 estimate.[16] However, 75 percent of patients with Alzheimer's disease are admitted to residential care within five years of diagnosis. If we could treat the symptoms of dementia more efficiently, delay its onset, or even cure dementia, quality of life would greatly improve both for patients and their family members.

HISTORICAL CONTEXT

In his 1726 book *Gulliver's Travels*, English author Jonathan Swift described how dementia affected the Struldbruggs— "Immortals" who lived forever but became progressively demented with age:

> ...they grew melancholy and dejected....When they came to four-score years,...they have no Remembrance of

anything but what they learned and observed in their Youth and middle Age, and even that is very imperfect…The least miserable among them appear to be those who…entirely lose their Memories.

At Ninety, they forgot the…Names of persons, even of those who are their nearest Friends and Relations. For the same Reason they never can amuse themselves with reading, because their Memory will not serve to carry them from the beginning of a Sentence to the end….

They were the most mortifying Sight I ever beheld…my keen Appetite for Perpetuity of Life was much abated.

Dementia, or "feeble-mindedness," related to old age has been known throughout history. The oldest descriptions of chronic forgetfulness in older populations occurred in Egypt in the ninth century B.C. The Roman surgeon Claudius Galen (130–200 A.D.), who mainly treated Roman gladiators, made the first physical description of age-related forgetfulness.[18] Throughout history, there have been scattered descriptions of problematic behavior and other symptoms in elderly people. The average life expectancy remained low for most of the Middle Ages (500–1500); it was rare for people to live to be 50 years old. If old people developed disturbing dementia symptoms, they were generally hidden away in their families' homes. If their behavior became too difficult to control, they were locked up in mental asylums. The behavioral symptoms of dementias were not understood as being separate from behavioral problems caused by other illnesses. In the 17th century, dementia or senility was seen as an inevitable part of the aging process that generally made people insane. It was often considered the work of witches and the devil.

French psychiatrist Jean Esquirol (1772–1840) provided the first modern description of dementia. In his classic early 19th-century work *Mental Maladies: A Treatise on Insanity*, he defined dementia: "A cerebral affection usually chronic...and characterized by a weakening of the sensibility, understanding, and will." He studied more than 300 patients and described the noncognitive symptoms of dementia, including hallucinations, delusions, aggressive behavior, and motor abnormalities. Among the causes for dementia, he mentioned not only aging but also head trauma, syphilis, and alcohol abuse, as well as "menstrual disoders, disappointed affections and political shocks."[10] Interestingly, in the 1830s French physicians first paid attention to the fact that the cognitive changes seen in the elderly might be caused by something that is different from the causes of mental retardation or insanity. They based their thoughts on the fact that age-related changes had not always been present in the patients, whereas mental retardation was present usually from early childhood, and insanity generally started in early adulthood.

It was not until 1907 that scientists had evidence to separate behavioral changes in the elderly as a separate condition from other mental illnesses. Dr. Alois Alzheimer, a German physician (1864-1915), first described what he actually saw in the brain tissue and correlated it to the behavior seen in dementia syndromes in 1907. He described what he found in the **autopsy** of the brain of a deceased demented 51-year-old woman. She had showed early onset symptoms of dementia and died four years later in the asylum where Dr. Alzheimer worked. When she was hospitalized, she had symptoms of disorientation, impaired memory, paranoia, and trouble reading and writing. She had become more and more unable to care for herself at home and resisted any help. As her symptoms gradually worsened, she also developed hallucinations and loss of higher mental functioning. He was the first scientist to make a connection between irreversible changes in the brain and dementia symptoms. In 1907, Dr. Alzheimer described in a German Medical journal his famous first case of the new disorder. The excerpt below describes some characteristic symptoms of the disease that this patient exhibited. It was translated by L. Jarvik and H. Greenson and published in the 1987 article "About a peculiar Disease of The Cerebral Cortex" in *Alzheimers Disease and Associated Disorders.*

"If one shows her objects, she usually names them correctly. Immediately thereafter, however, she has forgotten everything. When speaking, she frequently uses phrases indicating perplexity or embarrassment, or single paraphasic expressions (milk pourer instead of cup) sometimes one observes that she is completely at a loss of words. She clearly does not grasp some questions, and it seems that she no longer knows the use of certain objects."

After the woman died, Alzheimer noticed in the autopsy that her brain had some unusual features. Her **cerebral cortex** (the surface layer of the brain) was thinner than normal, and he also described "**senile plaques**" and "**neurofibrillary tangles**." These are still the criteria that we use to diagnose Alzheimer's disease after a person is dead. We have not advanced that much from Dr. Alzheimer's times in the way we diagnose this disease. Alzheimer's disease still cannot be definitively diagnosed until someone is dead and an autopsy has occurred.

For years, Alzheimer's disease was considered a **presenile dementia**, or a dementia of normal aging that started too early. Scientists were confused because in the brains of some elderly people without dementia, when examined after death, they found plaques and tangles, and some elderly people with dementia had few plaques and tangles in their brains. It wasn't until the late 1960s that scientists understood that the degree of dementia is related to the number of plaques. This means that there has to be a certain amount of brain changes before a diagnosis of Alzheimer's disease can be made, because part of normal aging includes that some plaques and tangles are seen in the brain. More discussion of plaques and tangles can be found in Chapter 4. During the 1960s, other causes of dementia were also recognized, which has helped scientists better understand the complexity of the dementia syndrome.[19]

At the time the woman described by Dr. Alzheimer lived, dementia was rare. As the life expectancy of humans has

Who Was Alois Alzheimer?

Alois Alzheimer was born in 1864 in Markbreit, Germany. He studied medicine and graduated in 1887 at the age of 23. The next year, he started his education in psychiatry and devoted himself to his great interest, neuropathology, the study of diseases of the nervous system. He worked with the famous German neruropathologist and psychiatrist Franz Nissl, who had developed a tech-

Figure 1.7 Alois Alzheimer. © *National Library of Medicine*

nique for staining proteins for research to investigate the normal and pathological anatomy of the cerebral cortex.

increased and the population gets older, dementia is becoming a huge national health problem. The knowledge and understanding of the causes of dementia have grown, but being able to prevent the onset of dementia would have an enormous impact not only on the public health-care system but on the quality of life for people who suffer from dementia and their caregivers. This makes dementia an urgent research priority and a crucial topic to learn about for all of us.

While working at the asylum, Alzheimer cared for a patient called Auguste D, who was 51 years old and had been suffering from dementia for five years. She had symptoms of progressive dementia, including amnesia, paranoia, and confusion. She died four and a half years later, and Alzheimer performed an autopsy. He studied her brain tissue under the microscope and realized that there were significant differences between her brain and normal brains. He was the first person to describe "senile plaques" and "neurofibrillary tangles" in the brains of people with dementia. He continued to study this new disease, which is named after him.

Alzheimer is also famous for describing brain changes in atherosclerosis, syphilis, and epilepsy, as well as the loss of nerve cells in Huntington's chorea. He worked at the universities of Heidelberg and Munich. In 1912, he was appointed professor of psychiatry and director of the Psychiatric and Neurologic Institute at the University of Breslau. Alzheimer died at the age of 51 in 1915 as a result of cardiac failure following endocarditis, an infection of the heart.

2 Signs and Symptoms of Dementia

My wife's first symptoms of Alzheimer's disease started in a very subtle way. One day she was looking around for something in the house and I asked her if I could help.

She responded that she needed the "picture box" but couldn't find it.

I wondered if she meant the computer or the television, but she stated that what she was looking for was something that made pictures. I asked her to describe how the thing she was looking for looked like. She stated that it looked like a box of nails. While I was getting very alarmed about her inability to name and describe what she was looking for, I finally realized that she meant the camera.

At that point I knew something was terribly wrong. I suggested to her that she should see a doctor but she didn't think anything was wrong with her. I shared my worries with our daughter, who also had noticed changes in her mother's behavior recently. After that, it was easier to convince my wife to have a physical exam by a doctor. The doctor did a thorough physical and neurological exam and ordered several additional tests including a brain scan and blood tests. We had to wait for more than a month before we received any answers. When our doctor finally called and told us that the diagnosis was Alzheimer's disease, probably in its very early stages, I was devastated.[18]

DIAGNOSING DEMENTIA

Diagnosing dementia can be complex and challenging. It can take a long time from the first suspicion that something is wrong to the diagnosis, since the symptoms often start as mild memory problems and progress slowly. It is important to distinguish between different types of dementia because the treatment can vary significantly. There are also rare conditions caused by medical or psychiatric illnesses, or drug reactions that are dementia-like but actually are not true dementia. They can often be reversed with treatment. A specific diagnosis will help the doctor predict the progress of the specific type of dementia and help the family choose treatment and prepare for what to expect as the illness progresses.

What is "Cognitive Functioning?"

Dementia refers to the loss of intellectual and cognitive functioning due to changes in the brain. Cognition is the mental process involved in knowing, learning, and understanding things, and cognitive means "relating to the mental process of learning." Cognitive functions that might be affected by dementia are:

- decision-making/judgment
- memory
- spatial orientation
- thinking/reasoning
- verbal communication
- neglect of personal safety, hygiene, nutrition

WHAT HAPPENS IN THE DOCTOR'S OFFICE

The first thing a doctor does is take a complete medical history. This is best done alone with the patient and then with someone close to the patient who can verify some of the symptoms and problems if the patient's memory is no longer reliable. It is important for the doctor to know of all medications that the patient is taking and for what conditions they are being used. Even past problems, such as head injuries, loss of consciousness, or serious infections of the nervous system, need to be described in as much detail as possible. The doctor also needs to know if there are any health problems that run in the family or if anyone in the family has suffered from dementia. The doctor will also want to find out what, if any, recent changes in the patient's general behavior or personality have been noticed or experienced.

As part of the evaluation, the doctor asks questions related to memory function, such as "What day is it today?", "Who is the president of the United States?", "Where are we?", or "Can you recite the alphabet?" Other questions relate to everyday tasks like paying bills and balancing a checkbook, preparing meals, or driving a car.

To help detect dementia, physicians often use screening tests that can be administered in the office. The most commonly used test is called the Mini-Mental State Examination (MMSE). A poor score on a test is suggestive of a dementia but does not alone warrant a diagnosis, since other types of brain conditions can alter a person's performance on this test.

In addition to a careful physical examination and screening tests, a physician will run a battery of blood and other tests to rule out any possible treatable causes of dementia. It is important to assess the patient's nutritional status, blood pressure, and the health of his or her heart. A careful neurological exam is done to rule out conditions like Parkinson's disease. Blood and urine tests to check for drugs and alcohol, or high levels of heavy metals, may need to be performed since all these substances can change cognitive functioning.

Sometimes depression can look like dementia, and it frequently happens at the same time as dementia. Depression can be diagnosed by asking specific questions related to mood and can be treated with antidepressant medications and psychotherapy. Thyroid hormone malfunctioning can be present with symptoms that look like depression and dementia. Deficiency in the hormone causes continual tiredness, slow speech, weight gain, cold intolerance, and muscle weakness. A simple blood test will tell the doctor how the patient's thyroid gland is working. The condition is treatable with thyroid hormone supplementation. Blood tests can also detect infectious diseases like HIV and syphilis, which can cause dementia-like symptoms. Deficiency of some vitamins, especially the group B vitamins, can cause cognitive dysfunctions. Other blood tests may be indicated based on the patient's family and medical history. Often a brain scan like **computed tomography (CT)** or **magnetic resonance imaging (MRI)** is performed to rule out strokes, tumors, or normal pressure hydrocephalus (NPH). In NPH, increased pressure in the brain and enlargement of the fluid-filled cavities in the brain cause specific dementia-like symptoms. Sometimes a brain scan will verify the NPH dementia diagnosis, especially if changes like cortical atrophy, or withering of brain cells on the cortex (the surface of the brain), indicates that the brain has shrunk.

WHAT IS THE BASIS FOR THE DIAGNOSIS?

To be diagnosed with dementia, the patient must have problems with memory. However, memory problems alone do not warrant a diagnosis of dementia. Certain types of memory problems are part of normal aging. This topic is discussed later in

Ten Warning Signs of Alzheimer's Disease

The Alzheimer's Association has come up with a list of 10 warning signs of Alzheimer's disease that may help people more easily recognize the condition. These warning signs are meant to serve as a guide for people to recognize common signs of Alzheimer's disease. Some of these symptoms may be present in other types of dementia as well, and are not necessarily predictors of Alzheimer's disease. If someone you know fits into some of these symptoms, he or she may need to be evaluated by a physician.

1. *Memory loss.* This is one of the most common early signs of dementia. It can also be present with normal aging. Patients with Alzheimer's disease have more severe memory problems. They may not only forget what to buy at the store but also to pay for their items when leaving the store. They may even forget entirely why they went to the store.

2. *Difficulty performing familiar tasks.* Patients with Alzheimer's disease may forget in what order to prepare a meal, or how to use the washing machine or vacuum cleaner.

3. *Problems with language.* Although it is normal to forget a word now and then, in Alzheimer's disease, people often forget simple words and may use moreunusual words that make their speech or writing difficult to understand.

4. *Disorientation to time and place.* With a busy schedule, it is normal to occasionally forget the date or the day of the week. People with Alzheimer's disease may forget where they are or how they got there. They may

even forget how to get back to their bedroom at night after a visit to the bathroom.

5. *Poor or decreased judgment.* People with Alzheimer's disease may dress inappropriately for the weather—for example, not wearing a coat in the winter or wearing heavy clothing on a hot summer day. They may also undress publicly as a response to feeling hot.

6. *Problems with abstract thinking.* Patients with Alzheimer's disease may lose the ability to understand addition and subtraction or even what numbers represent. This makes tasks like balancing a checkbook or understanding a timetable impossible.

7. *Misplacing things.* People with Alzheimer's disease not only forget things like where they placed their keys but frequently put them in unusual places like the freezer or oven.

8. *Changes in mood and behavior.* People with Alzheimer's disease do not only have normal mood changes like sadness or elation, but may have rapid and violent mood swings. They may have emotional outbursts with extreme anger and shouting, but then suddenly change to tears.

9. *Changes in personality.* People with Alzheimer's disease may change from being cheerful and outgoing to irritable and suspicious or timid and fearful.

10. *Loss of initiative.* We all get tired of our chores at times. In Alzheimer's disease, people lose interest even in important things. They may become passive, sit in front of the television, sleep more than usual, and may not want to engage in their usual activities.

this chapter. When a doctor evaluates a patient for possible dementia, he or she relies on the laboratory data, information from brain scans, and results from physical and neurological exams, as well as the clinical interview. According to the *Diagnostic and Statistical Manual,* to be able to diagnose dementia, the patient must have deficits in memory and at least one of four cognitive disturbances. These four cognitive problems are called **aphasia, apraxia, agnosia,** and **impaired executive functioning.** These cognitive problems reflect damage to the cortex of the brain, which processes information from other parts of the brain as well as from various parts of the body and peripheral nervous system. Finally, the patient's problems must interfere with social and occupational functioning to qualify as dementia.

MEMORY

Memory problems are often the first sign of dementia. It can be difficult to tell the difference between normal age-related memory problems and those caused by dementia. Examples of normal forgetfulness would be forgetting what you were supposed to buy at the store or having problems remembering phone numbers. If other cognitive functions are intact, it is easy to compensate for this forgetfulness by writing yourself notes or using visual cues to memorize items. With dementias, on the other hand, memory gradually gets worse and other symptoms develop. Usually, but not always, memory problems come first. Once the dementia progresses, one or more of the four cognitive deficits appears.

APHASIA

Aphasia is a loss of language skills, characterized by an inability to express oneself. Aphasia impairs regular communication. A person might have trouble repeating words or phrases, or understanding what others are saying. For example, a person might be unable to repeat a phrase like "no ifs, ands, or buts," be unable to find the exact words to name an object such as a pen or a watch, or have difficulty saying the date or following requests.

APRAXIA

Apraxia means that even though all muscles and joints are intact, the person is unable to perform physical tasks. Because of damage to specific areas of the brain, the patient's brain cannot appropriately process the spoken information and transform it into action. For example, a person might not be able to comb his or her hair, salute, wave good-bye, or brush the teeth when asked to mimic this behavior.

AGNOSIA

In agnosia, patients are unable to recognize or identify objects through touch even though their sensory functions are intact. For example, a person might not be able to recognize an object like a coin or a key by just feeling it with his or her hand. Instead, he or she needs to look at it to be able to recognize it.

EXECUTIVE FUNCTIONING

Impaired executive functioning refers to intellectual malfunctioning of activities, which are coordinated in the prefrontal cortex of the brain. They include disturbances in activities, such as planning, problem-solving, reasoning, judgment, organizing, sequencing, and abstracting. These activities are sometimes called higher brain functioning. For example, when patients are asked to tell what the proverb "Don't cry over spilt milk" means, they might respond, "You should just clean it up." Or they might have difficulty expressing specific similarities and differences between apples and oranges (both are round but have different colors). Patients may have loss of language skills, which shows up as problems finding words to express themselves. Patients may become disoriented and confused because of an inability to plan and organize, and they may experience a decline in the ability to perform routine tasks.

SOCIAL AND OCCUPATIONAL FUNCTIONING
For a diagnosis of dementia, the symptoms have to cause significant impairment on the levels of social and occupational functioning, impairment that is clearly a change to the worse from the patient's previous level of functioning. The symptoms of dementia have to interfere with everyday tasks at home and work that were not previously a problem.

ADDITIONAL SYMPTOMS
In addition to some of the symptoms described above, when dementia progresses, patients may neglect personal safety, hygiene, and nutrition. They might wander away from their home at night, unable to find their way back. Most people with dementia remain alert and aware until late in the course of the disease. This means that they pay attention and respond to their surroundings even though they may not understand what is going on. They may have personality changes, difficulty maintaining control over their emotions, and behavioral problems such as agitation, anxiety, **delusions** (when a person wrongly believes something and cannot be convinced otherwise) and **hallucinations** (seeing, hearing, and feeling things that are not there). Later on, patients might not be able to be cared for at home because of aggressive behavior, wandering, or getting easily lost in even familiar surroundings. When patients reach the end stage of dementia, they often have problems moving and keeping their balance or even getting out of a chair. Eventually they are confined to bed.

PHYSICAL SIGNS OF DEMENTIA

Alzheimer's disease typically has few physical abnormalities until the very end stage. Vascular dementia can have stroke-like deficit symptoms depending on which brain region has been affected. For example, patients may be unable to move their arm or leg on one side of their body. Dementias related to involuntary movement disorders like Parkinson's disease and Huntington's disease have symptoms of **chorea** (involuntary movements that look like dancing), tremor, and other physical symptoms that are characteristic of the two diseases.

If you have noticed someone close to you who is 65 or older having repeated problems with reasoning, language, planning, or memory, or if you find the person to be uncharacteristically forgetful and having a hard time making decisions, you need to suggest that the person have a complete physical checkup. A doctor can rule out any other illnesses that may be causing symptoms similar to dementia. Some changes in memory and thinking skills are typical as people age, but since memory problems and confusion can be caused by treatable factors, it is important to have a correct diagnosis.

DEMENTIA AFFECTS NEURONS

The brain is made of about 100 billion nerve cells, called neurons. A neuron has a cell body, an axon, and several dendrites. The axon extends out of the neuron and sends messages to other neurons. The dendrites also branch out of the neuron to receive messages from the axons of other neurons. Information travels though the neuron by electrical impulses. A covering over the axons, called a myelin sheath, speeds up the impulse. Once it reaches the tip of an axon, it is transmitted outward via chemical messengers, called **neurotransmitters**, through a tiny space called the synapse, to the next dendrite or cell body. These neurotransmitters bind to receptors at the receiving end of a

Brain Imaging

The only way to make a definite diagnosis of dementia is to look at the brain tissue under a microscope after the patient has died. Before then, a careful clinical exam and certain new imaging techniques can help diagnose dementias. The most common imaging techniques used to help diagnose or assess dementia are computed tomography or CT and magnetic resonance imaging or MRI. A positron emission tomography or PET scan is a newer technique that is increasingly used in research and diagnosing dementias.

CT scans use X-rays to see many layers of brain tissue. CT can detect any structural abnormalities like brain tumors. In dementia, the CT scan usually shows nonspecific cerebral atrophy (loss of brain tissue). Studies done over a period of years often show a rapidly progressing but nonspecific atrophy. Since nonspecific atrophy can be seen with various brain conditions, CT alone cannot diagnose dementia. However, it is relatively easy to administer, is quick and cheaper than MRI, and rules out many structural problems.

MRI scans use powerful electromagnets to create signals that are converted by computers into detailed brain images. An MRI shows more details than a CT scan. In patients with dementia, an MRI shows progressive atrophy first in the hippocampus, then in the temporal and parietal lobes, and then eventually in the frontal lobes. An MRI is more difficult to perform than a CT scan, since it takes about 40 minutes and the patient has to lie very still throughout the process.

A PET scan uses short-lived radio-labeled water or glucose to measure blood flow and glucose metabolism throughout the brain. It provides a rough picture of the brain's metabolic activity, chemistry, and physiology. In about one-third of patients with Alzheimer's, PET scans show decreased areas of cerebral oxygen and glucose metabolism in parts of parietal and temporal lobes.

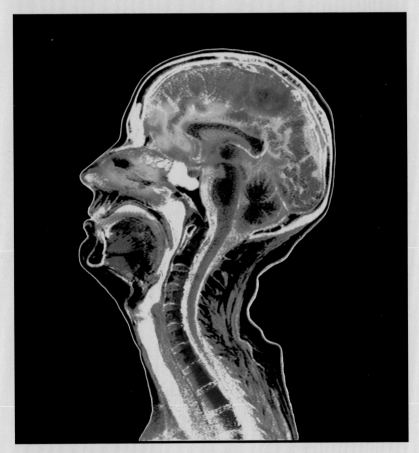

Figure 2.1 Brain atrophy has affected the area of the upper cerebrum, colored dark red in this magnetic resonance imaging scan of the brain of a 51-year-old man. © *S. Fraser/Photo Researchers, Inc.*

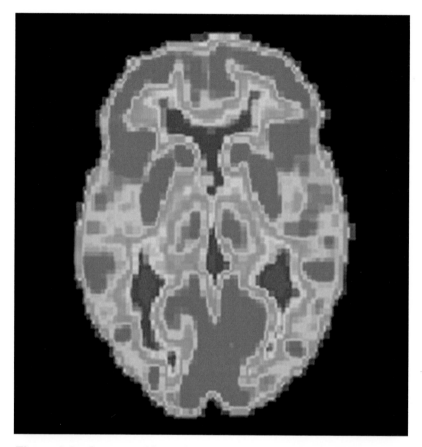

Figure 2.2a Compare this positron emission topography (PET) scan of a normal brain with a PET scan of a brain afflicted with Alzheimer's disease (Figure 2.2b, facing page). *Alzheimer's Disease Education and Referral Center, a service of the National Institute on Aging*

dendrite, where they trigger chemical reactions that tell the receiving neuron what to do. The neurotransmitter can either inhibit the function of a neuron or activate it by generating another electrical impulse that travels through the receiving neuron. Each neuron can have up to 15,000 synapses and during any moment millions of these signals are transmitted through neurons.

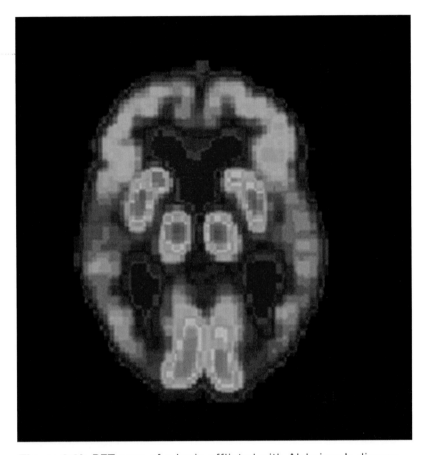

Figure 2.2b PET scan of a brain afflicted with Alzheimer's disease. *Alzheimer's Disease Education and Referral Center, a service of the National Institute on Aging*

Different brain regions possess groups of neurons that have highly specific jobs. Most form local circuits within a brain region. Some communicate with other brain regions. All this activity requires lots of energy, which the neuron receives through blood vessels as glucose and oxygen. For a healthy lifespan a neuron, which can live up to 100 years old, also needs to be able to repair and remove waste products. Damage to neurons can contribute to dementia.

DEMENTIA AFFECTS DIFFERENT REGIONS OF THE BRAIN

The human brain is divided into two cerebral hemispheres, the cerebellum, and the brain stem. The cerebral hemispheres are connected by a structure called the corpus callosum, which allows the left and the right side of the brain to communicate. The outer layer of the cerebral hemisphere is called the cortex. The cerebral hemisphere is divided into four regions: the frontal, temporal, parietal, and occipital lobes. The cerebellum is in charge of balance and coordination. It processes information from the eyes, ears, muscles, and joints, then communicates it to the rest of the brain and spinal cord to tell the body how to move. The brain stem is vital for survival. It connects the brain with the spinal cord and controls automatic functions that keep us alive, like blood pressure, heart rate, and breathing.

The brain regions affected by dementias are located both in the outer layers of the brain, the cortex, and in deeper structures of the brain. The cerebral cortex is the area of the brain where many cognitive functions like thinking, learning, speaking, remembering, and making decisions take place. The different regions of the cerebral cortex communicate with each other through neural circuits made out of neurons, but also with other brain centers located deeper in the brain tissue.

Some of these centers, which play a role in dementia, are called the hippocampus, thalamus, and the limbic system. These brain regions are involved in the complex processes of memory functioning. The frontal lobe is the center for the executive functions of the brain like motivation, attention, sequencing, and planning. It is the region that determines how the brain acts on what it knows. Damage to this area can cause lack of inhibition, apathy, or irritability. The **hippocampus**, which is part of the temporal lobe, is important for learning and short-term and long-term memory. Scientists believe that short-term memories are converted into long-term memories for storage in other

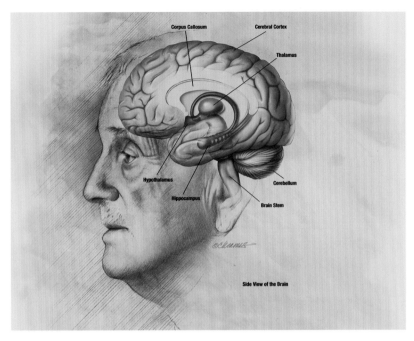

Figure 2.3 Side view depicting key areas of the brain. © *Neil Borden/Photo Researchers, Inc.*

brain regions. The **limbic system** is the home of the emotions and moods. Here strong emotional feelings are connected with strong physical reactions, like fear with a fast heartbeat. The limbic system influences how memories are formed. The **thalamus** is a center that receives information from the senses as well as information from the limbic system. It processes this information and sends it forward to various cortical regions. Damage to these areas of the brain can contribute to dementia.

3 Disorders Related to Dementia

In general, dementias are not curable. However, certain medical conditions have symptoms that look like dementia. Some other medical causes of dementia-like symptoms include high fever, dehydration, depression, drug reactions, electrolyte imbalance, vitamin deficiency, poor nutrition, medication reactions, thyroid problems, head injuries, and brain tumors. Certain emotions might result in dementia-like symptoms. Extreme sadness, depression, anxiety, stress, and even boredom might lead to forgetfulness, withdrawal, memory loss, and confusion. Treating underlying causes can reverse the symptoms of dementia or at least significantly improve them. Again, it is important to have a doctor make a careful assessment and diagnosis of the condition. In this chapter, we will look at some of the conditions that can be confused with dementia.

MENTAL RETARDATION

Mental retardation is a condition in which a person has below-average intellectual functioning and problems adapting to new situations. Sometimes mental retardation is confused with dementia, but they are two very different conditions. The major difference is that mental retardation is present from infancy or childhood. It does not change over time. Dementia patients, on the other hand, have lived a normal life and only develop their symptoms later in life. Patients with **Down's syndrome**, a disease caused by a **chromosomal abnormality** that causes mental retardation, often develop dementia of the Alzheimer's type in their early 30s or 40s, which is separate from their mental retardation. Mental retardation is a permanent state.

AMNESIA

Amnesia (loss of memory) is a condition that affects the memory but spares intellectual functioning. It is not a dementia but can sometimes be confused with it. Amnesia can occur as a postconcussion syndrome (after a head injury with loss of consciousness), after ECT (electroconvulsive therapy, used to treat severe depression), or after heavy alcohol use (either after one-time use or as a result of long-term use). Seizures can cause memory loss that lasts for a limited amount of time, and an infection of the brain called **encephalitis** can cause symptoms of amnesia. Typically patients with amnesia cannot recall events that have occurred recently and cannot remember newly presented information. Amnesia is a rare condition that sometimes is reversible.[11]

SUNDOWNERS SYNDROME

Sundowners syndrome is characterized by drowsiness, confusion, and accidental falls. It can be seen in older people who are overly sedated by certain medications. People over the age of 65 are generally more sensitive than young people to even small doses of medications that directly affect the brain, for example, sleeping pills, and are prone to develop this condition even if they do not have dementia. Symptoms are most obvious in the evenings or when the lights are out, thus the name Sundowners. This condition can also develop in patients with dementia if they are in unfamiliar settings—in a hospital, for example. These impairments can occur in darkened rooms when patients cannot use normal cues to help them understand where they are. Things like night lights, familiar belongings, clocks, or cal-endars, among other things, often help patients reorient to the present.[10] This syndrome, which is not a dementia but can eas-ily be mistaken for it, clears up when the causing agent or sit-uation is corrected.

NORMAL PRESSURE HYDROCEPHALUS

Normal pressure hydrocephalus (NPH) is a syndrome that has dementia as a symptom and it is sometimes reversible. It is a **clinical syndrome**. This means that the diagnosis is made based on three signs that can be seen during a physical exam: demen-tia, gait problem, and urinary incontinence. The typical gait problem involves a difficulty in starting to walk or turn, which makes patients seem clumsy and fall or trip easily. Urinary incontinence means that they cannot hold their urine and have to wear diapers.

Most often, NPH results from an unknown injury that caus-es **hydrocephalus**, an increase in pressure in the brain's fluid-filled cavities (ventricles). It is treated by **lumbar puncture**, which relieves the pressure. This treatment improves the patient's gait and urinary incontinence but not always the dementia. It is not clear why the dementia does not always respond to treatment. It is possibly due to earlier irreversible neuron damage. [11]

PSEUDODEMENTIA

In pseudodementia, a psychiatric disturbance causes dementia-like cognitive impairment. It is not considered a dementia. Most often, pseudodementia is caused by severe depression, but it can also be caused by anxiety or **schizophrenia**, a severe chronic mental illness. When examining patients with pseudodementia, doctors usually understand from patients' medical history that they have previously suffered or currently suffer from psychi-atric conditions rather than meet the criteria for dementia.

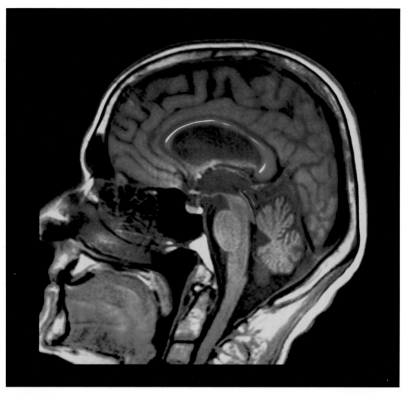

Figure 3.1 A side-view magnetic resonance imaging scan showing normal pressure hydrocephalus, an accumulation of fluid in the brain. © *Neil Borden/Photo Researchers, Inc.*

Treating the psychiatric condition will reverse or relieve the dementia-like condition.

DELIRIUM

Delirium is a condition that causes a change in the level of consciousness and attention. Patients can suddenly become disoriented, not know their name or where they are, or concentrate on any task. Other symptoms include inappropriate behavior and psychosis, including hallucinations and delusions. Symptoms can emerge within hours or days and fluctuate within a day.

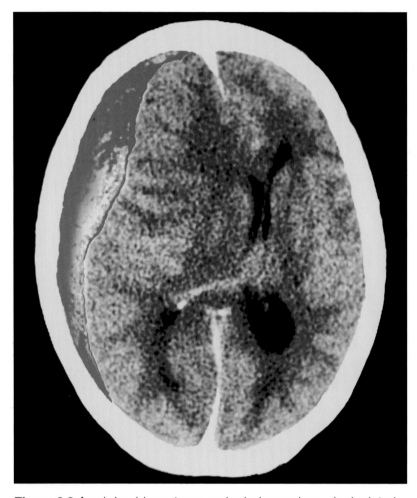

Figure 3.2 A subdural hematoma, or brain hemorrhage, is depicted in red (left) in this computed tomography (CT) scan. © *Zephyr/Photo Researchers, Inc.*

There may be moments when patients are clear in their thinking and seem to be their usual selves, but then deteriorate rapidly.

Delirium is easily misdiagnosed as dementia. Delirium, like depression, is common in patients with dementia. Causes include infections, dehydration, or overmedication. When the underlying cause is diagnosed and treated, symptoms usually disappear.

SUBDURAL HEMATOMA

This condition results from slow bleeding into the space between the skull and a protective tissue layer that surrounds the brain called the **dura mater**. People older than 65 are at risk for subdural hematoma mainly because their blood vessels are frail. Even a mild head trauma from a fall can cause this condition.

Symptoms of subdural hematomas include slow onset of headaches, change in personality, and dementia. Hematomas often cause minimal physical problems. Removal of the blood reverses the symptoms in most cases.

MILD COGNITIVE IMPAIRMENT

In recent years, researchers have become increasingly aware of a condition that they have named mild cognitive impairment (MCI). Aging is often considered to start between ages 45 and 65. With MCI, which does not fulfill the criteria of dementia, patients have memory complaints and measurable memory impairments for their age. All other functions are normal for their age. Researchers debate whether this condition should be treated or not, or if it is a pre-stage for dementia. Some but not all patients with MCI go on to develop Alzheimer's disease.

NORMAL AGING

Aging is a natural process and results in a variety of psychological, neurological, and physical impairments. Everyone ages differently. Normal aging can begin in some people at about age 45 but in most people it starts by age 65. Aging generally refers to the aging of cells. Structural changes take place in cells when we age, causing impairment and slowing of normal functions. It has been suggested that each cell has a genetically determined life span before it dies.

In his 2001 book *Clinical Neurology for Psychiatrists*, Dr. David Kaufman describes the "age-associated memory impairment,"

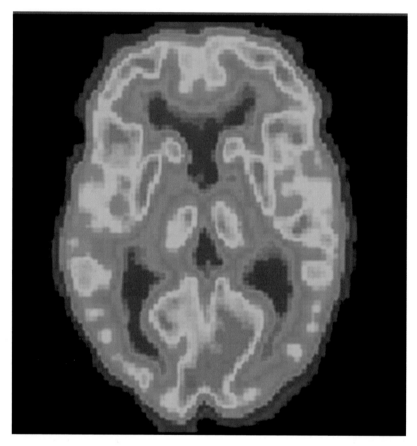

Figure 3.3a Comparison of a positron emission tomography (PET) scan of a 20-year-old brain (top) with a PET scan of an 80-year-old brain (see Figure 3.3b). *Alzheimer's Disease Education and Referral Center, a service of the National Institute on Aging*

or "forgetfulness of old age," that is considered the most common age-related change. This normal occurrence is characterized by forgetting small details, facts, or people's names. It also makes learning, then recalling, lists of words difficult. Different from dementia, this kind of memory impairment is rarely incapacitating. People can compensate for it by writing lists or using clues to help them remember. It generally does not affect a

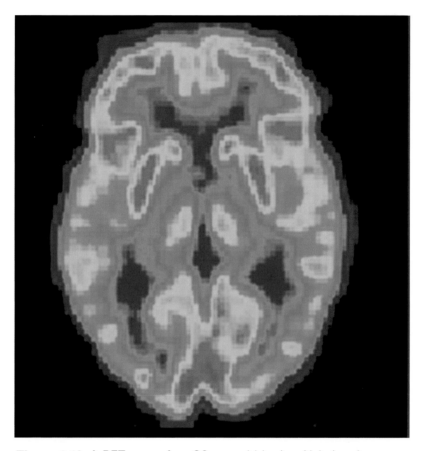

Figure 3.3b A PET scan of an 80-year-old brain. *Alzheimer's Disease Education and Referral Center, a service of the National Institute on Aging*

person's occupational and social functioning. However, in some people, it can progress to dementia.

Immune system changes in old age result in an impaired ability to fight off infections. It can take an old person longer than a young person to recover from a simple cold or flu. Normal age-related changes include not sleeping as well. Aging also makes us more susceptible to **neoplasias,** or cancer growths.[20]

Older people can lose muscle mass, developing muscle **atrophy** in the small muscles on the hands and feet. These changes lead to reduced muscle strength. Changes in reflexes, perception of vibration in the legs, and loss of balance make it hard for older people to stand on one foot with their eyes closed. These changes also contribute to a common walking pattern of older people. They tend to take short steps, bend their upper body slightly forward and not swing their arms as they walk. Many older people compensate for these changes by using a cane. Aging impairs the sense organs, causing hearing and vision problems and harming the sense of taste and smell. Hearing loss in older people can have many causes, from earwax buildup to stiffening of the eardrum to loss of neurons in areas of the brain associated with hearing.

Vision problems are also common in the elderly. Typical age-associated vision problems include poor focus and blurred or distorted vision. Color sensitivity to green, blue, and violet may be altered. Illnesses such as **cataracts** cause cloudy areas on the lens. The National Institute of Aging (NIA) has estimated that about 50 percent of Americans age 65 or older have cataracts.[21] Cataracts can be removed with surgery.

Some of the medications that the elderly often use, such as blood pressure medications, can cause a loss of the ability to taste as a side effect. The number of taste buds also declines with age, causing direct impairments in the ability to taste.

With increasing age, brain weight decreases to about 85 percent of what it once was. Other brain changes in the elderly include enlargement of the ventricles (the spaces in the brain that contain **cerebrospinal fluid**). Experts believe this change takes place because the cells that surround the ventricles die as part of normal aging, Widening of the **sulci** (grooves) on the surface of the brain is another age-associated change. Normal age-associated changes in the brain also include small amounts of **amyloid plaques,** and a limited number of neurofibrillary tangles, but are not indicative of Alzheimer's disease.

Not everything deteriorates with age. Interestingly, many cognitive processes remain unaffected by aging. Older people usually have little loss of vocabulary, reading comprehension, or general information. Verbal intelligence, executive abilities, most language skills and calculation abilities, and basic attention appear to be generally well maintained across the life span in healthy individuals.[21, 22] These facts also help to compensate for the age-associated memory impairments. In many cases and cultures, the accumulated life experience, education, and broad knowledge of older people gives them a respected position in the society and allows them to age with dignity.

Alzheimer's Disease

Mr. B is a 69-year-old man who runs a successful auto parts
business with his two sons. He has been in the business for 45 years.
He is well known for his phenomenal knowledge and memory of
parts for current American cars as well as those from the last 50
years. He has gained a reputation as an expert in the field of antique
cars and hobbyists consider his store one of the best in a large area.

However, over the last two years his sons have noticed that their
father's memory has started to fail him. He has increasingly been
having difficulty remembering details about the business and often
couldn't even recognize specific car parts. If the sons would joke
about his mistakes, he would become very irritated. He would
remind his sons that he still knows more about the business than
they do. His sons noticed also that their father was becoming more
withdrawn. Mr. B could not learn new things as he used to and
started to make troublesome mistakes. Once his poor memory
started to affect the business in a negative way, he could not par-
ticipate in the active work in the store. He became merely an
observer of his sons' work. All these changes were very painful for
his children to observe.[1]

BRAIN DETERIORATION OVER TIME

Mr. B's symptoms are typical of the most common type of the
dementia, **Alzheimer's disease**. Alzheimer's is a progressive **neurodegenerative** dementia that is associated with hippocampal
atrophy and loss of function of **cortical neurons** in the brain.

Progressive means that the symptoms get worse over time, and *neurodegenerative* means that the neurons in the brain fail. *Atrophy* means that the cells wither and shrink and ultimately lose their function and die. The gradual destruction of brain cells of a person with Alzheimer's disease causes the affected brain regions to wither and get smaller. The parts of the brain that control memory, logical thinking, and personality are generally the most affected. As areas in the brain become smaller, cavities form in the brain, fill with fluid, and become enlarged. This can be seen in diagnostic imaging studies of the brain like **MRI** or **CT scans**.

To make a definite diagnosis of Alzheimer's disease, a doctor would need to take a piece of the patient's brain and study it. It is impossible to diagnose Alzheimer's disease with 100-percent certainty without looking at brain tissue under a microscope. Because it is too dangerous to take a sample of brain tissue from a living person for an illness that has no cure, doctors instead make a probable diagnosis based on the patient's symptoms over time. To be diagnosed with Alzheimer's disease, patients need to have slow onset of dementia that gets worse over time. They also need to have results from blood tests and a physical exam that exclude other illnesses that could account for dementia.

Two types of Alzheimer's diseases (AD) have been identified based on the onset of symptoms: early onset and late onset. Early-onset Alzheimer's disease, which is very rare, appears to be inherited and has a strong genetic link. Symptoms can start in people as early as age 30 to 60. Late-onset Alzheimer's disease, which is the far more common type, does not appear to be similarly inherited. In this form of AD, a less strong genetic link exists but other factors including lifestyle, education and environmental factors play a role as well.

WHAT CAN WE SEE IN THE BRAIN?

In Alzheimer's disease, the nerve cells stop working because the illness disrupts three processes that keep the neurons healthy:

communication, metabolism, and repair. First, communication means that neurons can receive or send information, chemically or electronically from one neuron to another. Second, metabolism is a process in the neuron where energy is created for the neuron by breaking down nutrients or chemicals. It also includes the building of new compounds, like proteins, for its own use. Third, repair refers to the cleanup and removal of waste products and maintenance of the cells function. Problems in these three functions lead to the death of neurons, which causes problems with brain function and leads to the symptoms of Alzheimer's dementia.

When we use a microscope to look at the brain of a deceased person who suffered from Alzheimer's disease, two abnormal structures can be seen: **amyloid plaques** and **neurofibrillary tangles**. Some elderly people without dementia have small amounts of plaques and tangles in their brain. In Alzheimer's disease, however, there are many. Reduced cholinergic activity was detected about 20 years ago in the brains of people suffering from dementia. **Acetylcholine**, the main neurotransmitter (or chemical messenger) in the cholinergic system of the brain, is an important chemical messenger between neurons, which is involved in memory and learning. Reduced cholinergic activity means that there is too little of this substance in the brains of people with dementia. The currently available medications that treat symptoms of dementia work to increase the amount of acetylcholine in the brain.

AMYLOID PLAQUES

Amyloid plaques are made of a protein called beta-amyloid. Beta-amyloids are fragments of larger proteins called **amyloid precursor protein (APP)**. **Enzymes** called **secretases** act as scissors and cut these fragments from the APP. In a person with Alzheimer's disease, these fragments (beta-amyloids) clump

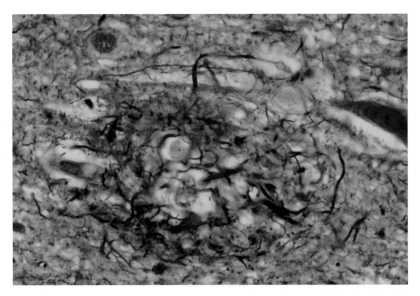

Figure 4.1 Senile plaques located in the gray matter of the brain of a person with Alzheimer's disease. © *Dr. Cecil H. Fox/Photo Researchers, Inc.*

together outside the neurons, forming plaques (also called amyloid plaques or beta-amyloid plaques). These plaques are most prominent in the brain regions that are important for memory, thinking, and decision-making. These regions include the hippocampus and temporal and parietal regions of the cerebral cortex. It is not clear what the normal function of APP is, but it appears that it may be important in helping neurons to grow and survive. It is also not clear whether the beta-amyloid plaques themselves cause Alzheimer's disease or whether they are just a byproduct of the illness. If the beta-amyloid plaques indeed are the cause of Alzheimer's disease, then it might be possible to treat patients by stimulating the immune system to destroy the beta-amyloids, or by inhibiting the secretase enzymes that cut the APP into beta-amyloid fragments. Many researchers are using these approaches to try to find treatments and a cure for Alzheimer's dementia.

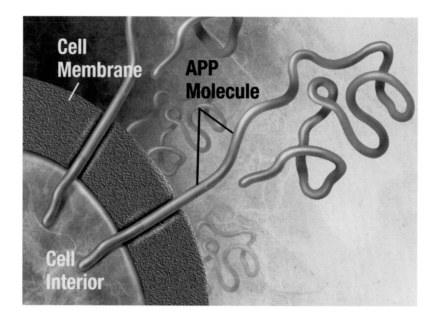

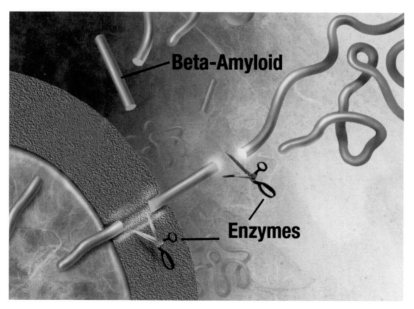

Figure 4.2a Amyloid precursor protein (APP) in the brain (top) fragment when enzymes cut them apart (bottom). *Alzheimer's Disease Education and Referral Center, a service of the National Institute on Aging*

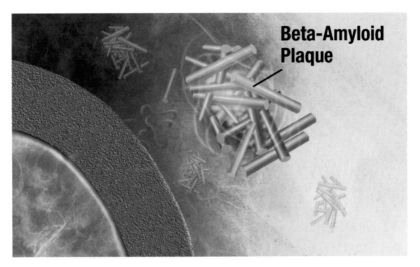

Figure 4.2b The accumulated fragments form plaques that interfere with brain function and are believed to be connected to Alzheimer's disease. *Alzheimer's Disease Education and Referral Center, a service of the National Institute on Aging*

NEUROFIBRILLARY TANGLES

Nerve cells have an internal skeleton, or support structure, that is partly made up of structures called microtubules. A microtubule is like a tiny tube that transports nutrients between different parts of the neuron. The **tau protein** makes the microtubules stable. In Alzheimer's disease, the tau protein seems to lose its ability to support the cell, which deforms and aggregates into neurofibrillary tangles. This leads the neuron's nutrient transport system to collapse, breaking down communication between neurons and eventually killing the cells.

CHOLINERGIC LOSS

More than 20 years ago, scientists discovered that patients with Alzheimer's disease had a deficit of a neurotransmitter called **acetylcholine**. This neurotransmitter has been shown to be important for memory, attention, and learning. Recognizing this deficit led to the development of medications called acetyl-cholinesterase inhibitors. These drugs inhibit the function of an enzyme called acetylcholinesterase, whose main job is to break down excess acetylcholine. By inhibiting this enzyme, the medicines increase the levels of the neurotransmitter acetyl-choline in the brain. In patients with mild to moderate symp-toms of Alzheimer's disease, memory and many other symp-toms improve with treatment of acetylcholinesterase inhibitors. Keeping stable amounts of acetylcholine in the brain does not cure Alzheimer's disease, but it can help improve the quality of life and delay the onset of more severe symptoms of Alzheimer's disease.

BEHAVIOR CHANGES IN ALZHEIMER'S DISEASE

Because Alzheimer's disease is a gradually progressive disease, three different stages can be recognized based on patient behav-ior and scientific studies in the brain. Although the rate at which symptoms emerge varies greatly from person to person, symp-tom development can be divided into mild, moderate, and severe forms.

It is not clear what causes Alzheimer's disease to start, but scientists have suggested that some changes in the brain may take place decades before the first symptoms are seen. Memory loss might be the first sign that Alzheimer's disease is developing. However, it is very difficult if not impossible to determine whether normal age-associated memory loss will lead to Alzheimer's disease.

MILD ALZHEIMER'S DISEASE

In the mildest form of Alzheimer's disease, memory loss contin-ues beyond normal age-associated memory loss, and patients cannot compensate well enough to avoid the inconveniences caused by memory problems. In this stage, scientists believe that

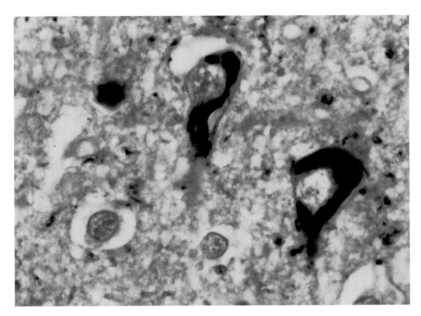

Figure 4.3 Two neurofibrillary (tau protein) tangles are visible in this section of a cerebral cortex. © *Pr. J.J. Hauw/ISM/Phototake*

amyloid plaques or neurofibrillary tangles (or both) have done some damage to neurons in the hippocampus. The cerebral cortex starts to be affected, too, evidenced by emerging changes in cognitive abilities. In a brain scan, it might be possible to see some shrinkage of the hippocampus and the cortex, and perhaps some enlargement of the ventricles.

The most typical clinical sign of mild Alzheimer's disease is memory loss. For example, patients have problems remembering people's names or where they placed an object. Other memory problems include forgetting appointments or conversations or forgetting to take medications. As confusion increases, patients may get lost even in familiar surroundings. It might take a person longer than usual to accomplish everyday tasks like laundry, shopping, preparing meals, or cleaning. Patients might get easily confused when they have to perform tasks where they have to integrate information from multiple sources, like when driving a car. The patient's orientation can be affected, too. For example, a person with Alzheimer's disease may forget how to get back to his or her bedroom after going to the bathroom at night. Alzheimer's disease patients might be unable to make plans for the future. They might neglect personal hygiene or how they dress, combining colors and styles in unusual ways. Poor judgment may lead them to make bad decisions and have trouble handling money and paying bills. Sadly, patients lose their spontaneity and sense of initiative. Their personalities may change, and they might become more edgy and behave in a hurtful way that is unusual for them. They might become argumentative, making it difficult for others to live with them. As a result of all these changes, a person who may look physically healthy starts to have trouble making sense of the world. This frightening experience may lead to increased anxiety and changes in mood.

MODERATE ALZHEIMER'S DISEASE

In moderate Alzheimer's disease, the damage to the brain continues to spread and affects areas in the brain that control language, reasoning, conscious thoughts, and sensory processing. The atrophy in the brain becomes more pronounced, as do the behavioral signs and symptoms of the disease.

Language can be affected and seen as vague, with repetitions, loss of vocabulary, and difficulty getting to the point in a description of story. Patients may have difficulty naming objects. This kind of language problem is called aphasia. A person with Alzheimer's dementia often has changes in personality at this stage. These changes can be especially difficult for the patient's family. Preexisting personality traits might be accentuated. For example, someone who has been shy with other people might get even more isolated. Patients may become less concerned about how their behavior affects other people. Patients with paranoid delusions often become hostile to their family members or caretakers. They might be irritable or explosive. About 20 to 30 percent of people with Alzheimer's dementia have hallucinations and 30 to 40 percent have delusions. The most common types of delusion are of the paranoid or persecutory type, where patients feel that others are trying to hurt them, and this feeling can make them hostile, fearful, and anxious. Dementia patients who also have psychotic symptoms commonly show physical violence and aggression. Having psychotic symptoms means patients have delusions and hallucinations and an inability to stay in touch with reality. Often at this stage, it is very difficult to manage patients at home and more intensive supervision and care become necessary. Wandering tends to be a particularly troublesome behavior at this stage. It is dangerous to the patients and difficult for the caregivers to handle.

Inappropriate behaviors may occur because patient's brains do not understand what they are being asked for, or the patient might not remember how to do a specific task. For example, undressing when the temperature is warm may seem reasonable to a patient with Alzheimer's dementia who doesn't remember that it is not acceptable to undress in public. Many patients with Alzheimer's disease constantly follow their spouse or caregiver and become extremely anxious when the person is gone. Sticking close to someone familiar may be the only way to bring some sense into the world for these patients.

SEVERE ALZHEIMER'S DISEASE

In this stage, the damage to the brain caused by plaques and tangles is widespread. Patients are completely dependent on others for care. The sense of self seems to have disappeared. Patients do not recognize family and are unable to communicate. They may lose bowel and bladder control. Sometimes they might even forget how to swallow solids. Sleep disturbances are common, as are

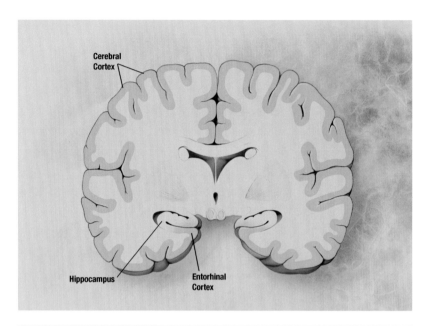

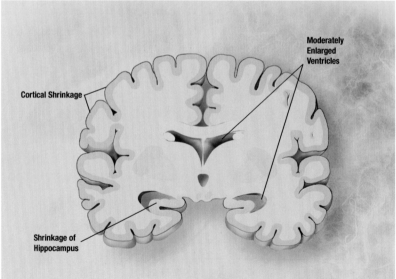

Figure 4.4a Three degrees of Alzheimer's disease: Preclinical Alzheimer's disease (top), mild Alzheimer's disease (bottom), and severe Alzheimer's disease (see Figure 4.4b, facing page). © *Alzheimer's Disease Education and Referral Center, a service of the National Institute on Aging*

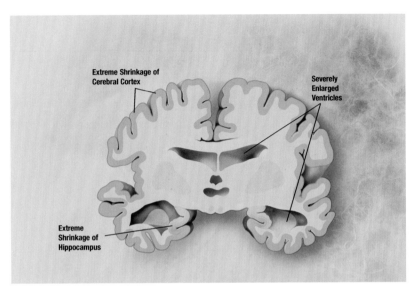

Labels on the figure:
- Extreme Shrinkage of Cerebral Cortex
- Severely Enlarged Ventricles
- Extreme Shrinkage of Hippocampus

Figure 4.4b Severe Alzheimer's disease. © *Alzheimer's Disease Education and Referral Center, a service of the National Institute on Aging*

aggressive outbursts and mood **lability** (instability of mood, or quick shifts from being happy to being sad to being angry).

Patients often have problems walking and keeping their balance because the plaques and tangles have damaged the area of the brain that controls movements. Even getting up from a chair can be difficult. Some patients develop seizures and skin infections, and have difficulty swallowing. In the late stages, they often lose muscle control and are bedridden most of the time. Vocal communication may be limited to groaning, moaning, or grunting.

At this stage, since the brain damage is so profound, some physical symptoms may emerge. Patients often develop what physicians call primitive reflexes. These are reflexes that every human being is born with for survival but disappear as we grow and mature and are not needed anymore to ensure survival. Some of these reflexes include the snout reflex and grasp reflex. The snout reflex occurs when someone taps the patient's upper lip with a finger. In response, the patient's lips purse and the mouth pouts. The grasp reflex occurs when the patient's palm is stroked crosswise. The patient responds by grasping the fingers of the person who stroked the hand and will not let go despite requests.[11]

Most people with Alzheimer's disease die from other illnesses, such as pneumonia. Aspiration pneumonia is common in people who have problems swallowing properly, causing them to breathe food or liquids or saliva into their lungs, which leads to infection in the lungs.

RISK FACTORS OF ALZHEIMER'S DISEASE

Scientists do not fully understand what causes Alzheimer's disease. It is likely that there are several factors that affect every person differently. The most common risk factor is age. The number of people with the disease doubles every five years beyond the age of 65.

Genes

Family history of Alzheimer's disease is a risk factor. Scientists believe that genetics play a role in many cases of Alzheimer's disease. The rare early onset form of Alzheimer's disease strikes between the ages of 30 and 60 and appears to be an inherited form of the illness. This form of Alzheimer's dementia seems to be related to mutations in the chromosomes 21, 14, 1, which lead to the production of abnormal proteins. The abnormal proteins have been named APP, **presenilin-1** and **presenilin-2**, respectively. Scientists believe that if a person inherits any damaged form of these three chromosomes, the early onset type of Alzheimer's dementia is almost guaranteed to develop.

It is likely that many genes play a role in increasing a person's risk of developing either early or late onset type of Alzheimer's disease. Studies have shown that people who have one parent with Alzheimer's disease have three times more of a risk of developing the disease than people whose parents do not have

Alzheimer's disease. A protein called **apolipoprotein E** (ApoE) is a product of a gene found in chromosome 19 and has been identified as a risk factor gene. We all have this gene, since it helps carry cholesterol in the blood. ApoE comes in many variants, or alleles, of which the ApoE e4 form has the highest likelihood of causing Alzheimer's disease.[14] The more common type of Alzheimer's dementia, late-onset Alzheimer's dementia, does also appear to have a genetic link. However, it is probably brought on by a combination of factors, including environmental, genetic and lifestyle risk factors.

Environment and Lifestyle

There are also environmental risk factors for Alzheimer's disease. An association between low education level and Alzheimer's disease has been suggested, but the exact reason for this is not clear. Some scientists believe it has to do with synaptic concentration (the amount of alternative routes a neuron can use to communicate with other neurons). The thought is that the higher your education level, the more synaptic connections your neurons have had to make in order to process all of the information stored in your brain; this has been called a cognitive or neurological reserve. This threshold model proposes that a more educated person might have more synapses to lose before behavioral problems show up or that they exhibit dementia only if their cognitive reserve capacity falls below a specific threshold. The accuracy of this approach is debated and some scientists believe that linguistic ability (as described in Chapter 7 in the Nun Study) may be a better marker for aspects of cognitive ability, or reserve.[23]

A new line of studies suggests a possible link between Alzheimer's disease and cardiovascular disease. A higher level of the amino acid **homocysteine** is known to be a risk factor for heart disease. It has also been shown to be a risk factor for Alzheimer's disease. The amount of homocysteine in the body can be reduced by increasing intake of folic acid, found in green vegetables.

Another cardiovascular risk factor is high cholesterol levels in the blood. Medicines called **statins** that are used to lower cholesterol have also been associated with lowering the risk of developing Alzheimer's disease.[24] Estrogen taken by women after menopause has been suggested to have some protective effect against Alzheimer's disease.[25]

Inflammation

Inflammation may play a role in the development of Alzheimer's disease. The amyloid plaques in the brains of Alzheimer's patients are often surrounded by cells that are activated by an inflammatory process in the body. However, it is not clear whether this has a good effect or a bad effect. Some scientists believe that inflammation promotes a cycle that is going to lead to cell death. Others believe it is the body's way of trying to remove the amyloid plaques. It has been speculated that people who take nonsteroidal anti-inflammatory compounds (NSAIDs, such as ibuprofen) may lower their risk for Alzheimer's disease.[26]

Head Injury, or Traumatic Brain Injury (TBI)

It appears that head injury increases the risk for Alzheimer's disease.[27] Traumatic brain injury (TBI) during adulthood has been considered a risk factor for Alzheimer's disease. This is supported by the fact that many former boxers who have experienced frequent head injuries often develop dementia later in life. This type of dementia has been named dementia pugilistica, or "punch drunk" syndrome. It typically causes symptoms similar to Parkinson's disease, as well as personality changes.[11] Scientists have not yet been able to determine whether TBI alone leads to Alzheimer's disease or if the person must also have a genetically inherited vulnerability to come down with the illness.

Other Types of Dementia

5

DEMENTIAS ASSOCIATED WITH ALZHEIMER'S DISEASE

Vascular Dementia

"Ms. M is a 57-year-old woman whose memory problems slowly *had become worse over the past couple of years. She was still able to function at home with the help of family and friends. However, about six months ago, she suddenly started having additional problems with walking and she was complaining that her right side of her body, particularly her foot, was feeling weaker. After some days she started having difficulties speaking clearly. Her alarmed family members urged her to have a physical exam. She was found to be generally healthy except problems with walking straight, leg weakness, unclear speech, and mildly elevated blood pressure."[1]*

Ms. M is suffering from the second most common type of dementia, vascular dementia (VaD). The high frequency of VaD makes sense when you remember that stroke and ischemic heart disease are the leading causes of death and illness among elderly people. In vascular dementia, symptoms are caused by one or several strokes. A stroke occurs when blood, for some reason, cannot get to one part of the brain. The lack of blood causes neurons to die. A stroke can be caused by a blood clot or a fatty deposit that blocks the blood vessels that normally bring oxygen and nutrients to the brain cells. People with cardiovascular disease, also called ischemic heart disease, or cerebrovascular disease

Dementia cues from walking style

Abnormal walking patterns in the elderly may be an early warning sign of dementia other than Alzheimer's disease, a new study shows.

Chances of developing dementia according to abnormal gait

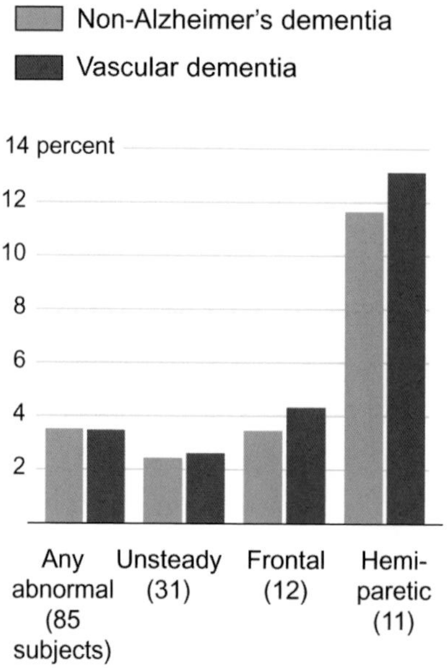

☐ Non-Alzheimer's dementia

■ Vascular dementia

14 percent

12

10

8

6

4

2

| Any abnormal (85 subjects) | Unsteady (31) | Frontal (12) | Hemi-paretic (11) |

Frontal gait characterized by short steps, wide base and difficulty picking feet off the floor.

Hemiparetic gait characterized by swinging the legs outward in a semicircle from the hip.

SOURCE: New England Journal of Medicine   **AP**

Figure 5.1 © *AP Images*

have a high risk of stroke. A stroke can also happen when a blood vessel in the brain bursts and causes bleeding into the brain. People who have high blood pressure are at risk of having a stroke. Other risk factors for VaD include diabetes, **hyperlipidemia** (high cholesterol levels in the blood), smoking, and being older than 65.

VaD can have either an abrupt or gradual onset. VaD can stay unchanged after the onset or worsen over time. This tells you about the variety of ways that strokes can affect the brain. The abrupt onset of dementia happens when the patient has a stroke in a specific brain region that is critical for intellectual functioning. Slow onset of VaD can follow several small strokes over a period of time if they take place in brain regions that are less important for functioning. More serious effects can occur from several small strokes if they continue to occur over a longer period of time and then cause a lot of damage to a brain region.

Patients usually have specific neurological signs and symptoms. For instance, they might have weakness on one side of their face or body, as Ms. M did in the example above. They may have problems using an arm or a leg or both, or problems with speech. This type of dementia appears to keep the normal personality intact, but patients may have nighttime confusion, depression, and emotional lability.

VaD symptoms usually start abruptly. Some of the following symptoms may be a sign of VaD:

- confusion and problems with recent memory
- wandering or getting lost in familiar places
- moving with rapid, shuffling steps
- loss of bladder or bowel control
- inappropriate laughing or crying
- difficulty following instructions
- problems handling money[28]

As you can see, most of the symptoms are similar to those seen with Alzheimer's disease.

Sometimes, the term *multi infarct dementia* is used to describe vascular dementia. Multi infarct dementia generally refers to the fact that several strokes cause the dementia syndrome. The brain is quite sophisticated in its functioning, however. VaD can be caused by only one strategically located stroke, or people can have several small strokes with little symptoms if the locations of the strokes are not critical for functioning. Some of the smaller strokes may even occur in brain regions that don't produce any symptoms. These are called silent strokes.

To diagnose VaD, doctors use the same criteria as they apply when diagnosing Alzheimer's disease and other dementias. They need to obtain a thorough medical history, physical evaluation, and neurological and mental status examinations. They also perform blood tests because some rare disorders can cause increased blood clotting and, thus, an increased risk of stroke. Specific signs of a stroke in the brain can be identified in a neurological exam and seen in a brain scan (CT or MRI scan). Doctors make a diagnosis based on all these tests, determining whether the patient has probable, possible, or definite VaD.

It is sometimes difficult to separate Alzheimer's disease from VaD. Scientists have also concluded that the two illnesses can often happen at the same time in the same person. A person can have Alzheimer's disease with atrophy and symptoms more typical for Alzheimer's, but also have visible marks of old strokes in the brain and some neurological symptoms. In such cases, it is difficult or even impossible to determine which form of dementia is the primary one.[29]

A transient ischemic attack, or TIA, is caused by a temporary blockage of blood flow to a part of the brain. Symptoms of TIAs are similar to strokes but they usually last only about 20 min-

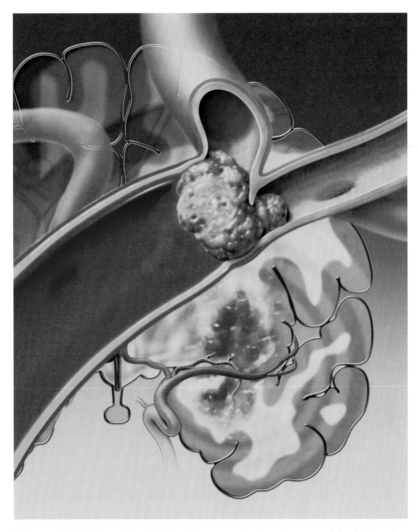

Figure 5.2 A blood clot lodged in a cerebral artery can block blood flow and cause a stroke. © *Bodell Communications, Inc./Phototake*

utes. People can experience slurred speech, dizziness, or mild weakness in an arm or leg. A TIA is a warning sign that the person is at risk of having a full-blown stroke. Medical attention is needed to find out the reason(s) for the blockage and start appropriate treatment to prevent a stroke.

At present, there is no effective medication or treatment for VaD. Prevention and management of the risk factors are the best way to battle this condition. Quitting smoking and controlling diabetes and high blood pressure have been shown to reduce the rate of strokes.[29]

LEWY BODY DEMENTIA

Dementia with **Lewy bodies** is a less common form of dementia. Some of the findings in the brains of patients with this type of dementia look a lot like those seen with Alzheimer's dementia. Patients with Lewy body disease (LBD) have some symptoms that appear similar to Alzheimer's dementia but also have symptoms that are different, such as fluctuating alertness and cognition, visual hallucinations and symptoms of Parkinson's disease. Patients with LBD often have less severe memory problems in the early stages of the illness and may have more problems with executive functioning (for example, planning and problem solving) than typically seen in Alzheimer's patients. Fluctuating cognition means that patients have quite dramatic shifts in their cognitive capacity from day to day, sometimes even hourly. Patients might be able to have a logical conversation with you but later in the same day seem to be incoherent, forgetful, or confused. In rare cases patients might even lose consciousness. Visual hallucinations are common. Patients often fall asleep easily during the day but have restless, disturbed nights with confusion, nightmares, and hallucinations.[30] The Parkinson's symptoms in this type of dementia include rigidity, stiffness, and slowing of movement. However, patients usually have less of the tremor typically seen in Parkinson's disease.

LBD is, sadly, quite dramatic. The time the symptoms first arise until death is shorter than with the typical course of Alzheimer's disease—about six to eight years.

After death, amyloid plaques typical of Alzheimer's disease are seen in the brains of LBD patients, but there are only few neurofibrillary tangles. There are plenty of so-called **Lewy bodies** concentrated mainly in the cortex but also in deeper brain structures that are important for regulating movement.

The brains of LBD patients also show a marked reduction in the levels of acetylcholine. Usually medications that increase the levels of acetylcholine are used and often have good effect, especially on the behavioral symptoms. It is very important to diagnose LBD correctly, since patients with this type of dementia may have a bad reaction to certain types of medications. Patients with this condition are extremely sensitive to conventional neuroleptic medications, which are usually used to treat schizophrenia, psychotic disorders, as well as anxiety, agitation, hallucinations, and delusions. In cases where patients have hallucinations and delusions, newer types of **antipsychotics** called atypical antipsychotics may be used, because they have fewer side effects and affect the brain in a different way than conventional antipsychotics. Patients with LBD may develop symptoms of depression and anxiety because of the frightening hallucinations. These symptoms can be treated with **selective serotonin reuptake inhibitor (SSRI)** antidepressants such as (paroxetin) Paxil,® (fluoxetine) Prozac,®, (sertraline) Zoloft.® or (escitalopram) Lexapro®.[11, 31]

FRONTOTEMPORAL DEMENTIA

Frontotemporal dementias (FTD) are degenerative brain disorders that specifically affect the frontal and temporal regions of the brain. These areas control functions such as reasoning, judgment, personality, social behavior, movement, speech, language, and certain aspects of memory.[32, 33] FTD is not as common as Alzheimer's dementia or vascular dementia. It accounts for perhaps 3 percent of all dementia cases. It typically occurs in people between the ages of 35 and 75, and it affects men and women equally.

FTD's effects are different from other dementias in that personality changes take place over a period of several years before other dementia symptoms occur.

The behavioral problems associated with FTD generally make the patient act uninhibited in socially inappropriate ways. For example, people might steal or eat with their fingers. Sometimes they display inappropriate sexual behavior, including asking people indecent questions. Some patients can become apathetic, whereas some can become hyperactive. Patients might stop paying attention to their personal hygiene and appearance, for example, by wearing dirty or torn clothes and not showering. Most people with FTD are unaware or unconcerned with their behavior. Patients can experience appetite changes and start to eat constantly, which causes weight gain. Sometimes patients develop oral fixation, meaning that they will put almost anything in their mouths. They behave like infants who explore the world by putting objects in their mouths. The speech and language problems that develop in some patients can be so serious that patients are left mute. Some sufferers display repetitive behavior, like collecting or hoarding things and washing their hands repeatedly.

FTD differs from many other dementias, including Alzheimer's, in that the memory is rarely affected in the early stages. When memory is affected, the problems are never as severe as with Alzheimer's disease.

FTD causes motor problems, mainly because the brain areas affected play a role in controlling many motor activities. Some patients become rigid in their movements or lose their balance. However, they do not develop the kind of tremor and rigidity that patients with Parkinson's dementia often have.

Researchers have come up with criteria to differentiate Alzheimer's disease from FTD. The symptoms are strikingly different. In FTD, the patient loses personal awareness, overeats, has self-preserving behavior, and goes through a loss of language skills.

The pathological changes in the brains of patients with FTD are not yet clear, and there is no cure for this devastating disease. However, scientists have recently discovered that there is an abnormal accumulation of tau proteins inside the nerve cells in the brains of FTD patients. The tau protein is part of the support structure in the nerve cell and serves as a transport system for nutrients and other molecules. In FTD, tau becomes abnormal and forms tangles that disrupt normal nerve cell processes and ultimately kills the cell. This happens mostly in the frontal and temporal brain regions. **Gliosis,** a scarring of tissues when neurons die, then can occur. A process where holes form in the outer layers of the brain called **vacuolisation** can result in some cases. Because some of the symptoms of FTD are quite unusual, diagnosis is difficult. FTD might easily be misdiagnosed as a psychiatric problem or Alzheimer's disease. It is important for a physician who is knowledgeable about various dementias to examine the patient. There is no treatment available to stop or even slow the process of FTD. However, some of the behavioral symptoms can be treated or alleviated by antidepressants or antipsychotic medications.

DEMENTIAS RELATED TO MOVEMENT DISORDERS
Parkinson's Dementia

Parkinson's disease is a progressive disorder of the central nervous system. Neurons in the basal ganglia region of the brain slowly lose their ability to produce a neurotransmitter called **dopamine**, resulting in the dysfunction of the basal ganglia, with motor symptoms such as tremors, stiffness of the limbs and joints, loss of motor control and **bradykinesia,** which is a decrease in spontaneous movements. The most disabling physical feature is the slowing of spontaneous movement, specifically, a "poverty" of movement, as doctors usually call it. It can be seen in patients' faces as "masked faces," where patients blink infrequently and have a blank, staring facial expression. The symptom that is noticed most often by other people is the tremor or shaking of hands when the person is at rest. Patients also have problems rapidly flexing their hips, spine, or knees, which makes it difficult to sit down in a chair. To observers, it looks like they fall into the chair like a stiff doll. Patients also have problems keeping their balance and they walk with short, shuffling steps. Medication is used to replace dopamine and control motor symptoms.

Not all people with this disease develop dementia, but it has been estimated that 20 percent of all people with Parkinson's disease develop dementia. Of patients older than 70, 40 percent develop dementia.

Typical symptoms of the dementia in Parkinson's disease include inattention, poor motivation, difficulty shifting mental sets (problems in transitioning from one activity or emotional state to another), and slow thinking. Memory problems tend not to be as severe as is seen in Alzheimer's disease, but they still impair the patient's functioning. Patients have problems with executive functioning like planning, organizing, and problem solving.

The cause of Parkinson's dementia is not clear. Many researchers believe that the dementia seen with Parkinson's disease is actually Alzheimer's disease. This view is supported by the fact that many demented patients (up to 35 percent) with Parkinson's disease have plaques and tangles in their brains, like those seen with Alzheimer's disease. However, to make the case more complex, not all patients with Parkinson's disease and dementia have these hallmarks of Alzheimer's disease in their brains, and some may have Lewy bodies.[11, 34]

Huntington's Disease

Huntington's disease is an inherited, progressive brain disorder. It usually begins during midlife and causes involuntary movements. Symptoms typically include chorea, personality changes, and dementia. Huntington's disease is also called Huntington's chorea because of the brief, jerky, brisk, purposeless, involuntary movements that are observed in patients with this disease, which look like a random "dance." *Chorea* is a Greek word for "dance." The movements typically occur in the limbs, face, or trunk. Initially, the movements are seen in the face and upper limbs as grimacing or frowning, fidgeting of fingers or shoulder shrugging. When patients try to walk, their gait is irregular, jerky, and looks uninhibited. Eye movements are often also affected.

Typically the symptoms of Huntingdon's disease, including cognitive changes, movement disorder, and personality changes, are all present at the onset of the disease. The movement distortions are often aggravated by strong emotions or just concentrating or walking. Involuntary movements can become so severe that the person cannot perform his or her normal daily activities. In more advanced stages, walking takes on a "stuttering" gait when the patient has problems with balance.

Personality and behavioral changes often occur, including irritability, apathy, violence, impulsivity, and emotional lability (moodiness), disorientation, and impaired judgment as well as memory and speech problems. Many patients suffer from depression.

Dementia symptoms also show up as memory disturbances with loss of detailed recollection, organization, and planning. As the disease progresses, the intellectual difficulties become more pervasive.

Huntington's disease can occur in juveniles. This type starts before age 15 and has slightly different symptoms than adult-onset Huntington's disease. In young people the symptoms resemble those of Parkinson's disease and cause seizures. The prognosis is grim, because it can quickly lead to death.

Today, the diagnosis of Huntington's disease can be confirmed by the presence of a particular genetic defect in chromosome 4. Before gene tests became available, doctors had to make the diagnosis based on the patient's symptoms.

There is no cure for this devastating disease. Treatment is based on trying to ease the symptoms.[11, 34] Patients usually live 15 to 20 years after the diagnosis. Patients usually die from pneumonia, trauma, or suicide. Pneumonia and trauma are usually a result from the uncontrollable movements in the body, which can cause accidental swallowing of food and fluids ending into the lungs, causing infection. Trauma often occurs as a result of accidents, including falls, burns, and traffic collisions. Since the prognosis is very grim and there is no cure, some people fall into depression, which, if left untreated, can lead to people taking their own life.

Wilson's Disease

Wilson's disease, also known as hepatolenticular degeneration, is a genetic illness caused by a defect in chromosome 13. The liver and the brain's lenticular nuclei (a structure deep in the brain that is involved in involuntary movements) are mostly affected. It typically includes dementia, with Parkinson's-like symptoms such as involuntary movements in older children and young adults and psychiatric problems.

This is a disease that, if detected and treated early, is reversible. Wilson's disease is caused when copper is not excreted sufficiently and is then deposited in various organs such as the brain, liver, and eyes. Normally copper is absorbed by the intestine and metabolized by cells, incorporated into cerulo-plasmin, or excreted into bile. Because of an abnormal accumulation of copper in the liver and eyes, cirrhosis or damaging copper deposits in the eye's cornea can result (seen as a specific green-brown pigment also called Kayser-Fleischer ring).

Usually symptoms first appear in patients between the ages of 10 and 25. Often the first symptoms are personality changes, behavioral disturbances, and cognitive impairment. Mood symptoms or thought disorders usually occur before problems with movement. Typical movement symptoms include rigidity, akinesia (lack of movement), Parkinson's-like symptoms and a wing-beating tremor. The name comes from the flapping movements made by the tremor of the arms and shoulders.

If this condition is diagnosed before permanent damage has taken place in the liver and brain, the symptoms can be reversed. A blood test showing elevated levels of serum cerulo-plasmin, the protein that normally carries copper, is diagnostic. The excess copper can be removed by a chelating agent, such as penicillamine, which binds to copper and is then excreted from the body.[11]

DEMENTIAS ASSOCIATED WITH INFECTIOUS DISORDERS

Infections of the central nervous system commonly cause dementia in older people, although it should be noted that these disorders can be infectious, not the dementias. Bacterial infections can cause meningitis (infection of the surface of the brain) or brain abscesses (pockets of infections). They start rapidly with symptoms of infection including high fever. They also lead to confusion and dementia-like symptoms. If the organism, bacteria or fungus, is diagnosed the condition can be treated with antibiotics.

Viruses can also cause infections of the brain that result in symptoms like those of dementia. Dementia symptoms often develop if the infection lasts for a long time. Symptoms are not always reversible. A virus called herpes simplex is particularly known for causing dementia-like symptoms, because it tends to sit in the temporal cortex, damaging this area and leading to dementia symptoms.

Infectious organisms called **prions** cause the very rare but fatal Creutzfeldt-Jakob disease. Mad cow disease is a known variant of this illness, usually transmitted to humans by eating meat from a cow that was infected by the prion. Symptoms of this type of dementia include memory problems, behavioral problems, and loss of coordination that leave patients wheelchair-bound. This disease progresses rapidly, with mental deterioration, involuntary movements, and eventually leads to death.

The human immunodeficiency virus (HIV) commonly causes dementia when it has developed into Acquired Immune Deficiency Syndrome (AIDS). Currently life expectancy for those infected with HIV or with full-blown AIDS can be extended by medication. In the AIDS stage of the HIV infection the body has been weakened by the virus, so that the body fails to protect the various organs in the body, including the brain, from attacks by simple bacteria and viruses. AIDS dementia is caused by direct HIV infection of the brain. It affects about 20 percent of all AIDS patients but becomes more common in the late stages of the illness. It is also more common in older patients and those who acquired the infection by intravenous (IV) drug abuse.

Typical features of the AIDS dementia include a rapid decline over weeks or months. The person has problems with concentration and memory, as well as apathy and withdrawal from social interaction. Sometimes early AIDS dementia can be confused with depression. Patients often have additional neurological symptoms like slowness of movement and a clumsy, slow gait. AIDS dementia is a serious condition. Usually 80 percent of

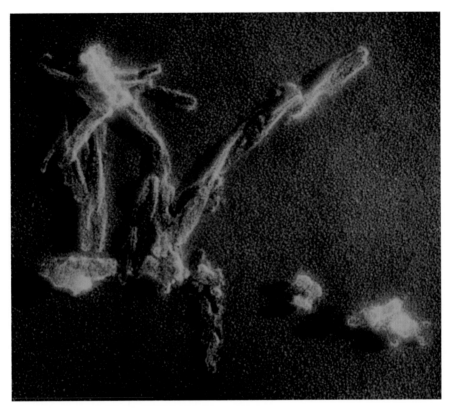

Figure 5.3 Color-enhanced electron micrograph of prions isolated from an infected hamster. These protein molecules are often found in direct connection with illnesses of the nervous system, such as mad cow disease. © *Eye of Science/Photo Researchers, Inc.*

those who don't immediately die lose most of their cognitive function. They are left with impaired movement and speech, incontinent, and severely demented.

SUBSTANCE-INDUCED PERSISTENT DEMENTIA

Substance-induced persistent dementias are caused by chronic alcohol abuse, inhalant use (for example, glue sniffing), halluci- genic drugs, or **sedatives** (for example, prescription antianxiety medications like benzodiazepines). These compounds are toxic to neurons when taken in large amounts, and can cause brain damage, dementia, or death.

Generally, chronic, excessive alcohol consumption leads to damage to neurons and cognitive impairment. The condition is usually called Wernicke-Korsakoff syndrome. It develops in 50 percent of all chronic alcoholics and begins with a general confused state, apathy, slowness, and indifference to problems. Distinctive symptoms are impaired memory of previously known facts as well as inability to remember new ones. Again, the memory problems alone are not enough to allow for a diagnosis of dementia, but as the condition progresses, other symptoms that resemble Alzheimer's dementia can develop. Patients typically have many neurological symptoms along with clear atrophy in the brain that can be seen with brain scans.

Other reasons that alcoholics develop dementia include head trauma because of the high risk of falling while intoxicated. Nutritional deficiencies can also contribute to the development of dementia. Lack of vitamin B_1, or thiamine, is known to result in dementia. In fact, not all people who develop Wernicke-Korsakoff syndrome are alcoholics. People who are lacking B_1, have undergone starvation, dialysis treatment for kidney failure, or chemotherapy for cancer treatment are at risk of developing it.[11]

Causes and Treatments of Dementia

CAUSES OF DEMENTIA

Most scientists believe that the key biological events leading to the symptoms of Alzheimer's disease include problems in communication between certain nerve cells in the brain and the death of these cells. Different theories exist regarding the exact cause of this cell malfunction and cell death. This has led to a lot of research trying to understand what initiates these events and how we might intervene. Finding the cause and the way to cure Alzheimer's disease is a challenging race in which many scientists are involved. Alzheimer's disease is probably caused by a complex series of events that take place in the brain long before the first symptoms develop. Most experts today think that genetics, lifestyle, and environmental factors all work together to cause Alzheimer's disease, and it appears that each of these factors may affect each individual differently.[17, 24]

THE AMYLOID HYPOTHESIS

The prevailing theory regarding the underlying cause of Alzheimer's disease is called the amyloid hypothesis. It suggests that abnormal processing of the amyloid precursor protein (APP) in the body causes Alzheimer's disease. This protein is found throughout the body but its normal function and purpose is still unknown. Like many proteins, APP goes through stages of processing during which it is cut into different functional segments.

Abnormal cutting of the APP produces a fragment known as **beta-amyloid**. Enzymes called secretases cut the APP into these beta-amyloids. These fragments then group together to produce the amyloid plaques that are found in the brains of people who have died of Alzheimer's disease (these are also called amyloid plaques or beta-amyloid plaques, which can be seen in the brain of people with AD with a microscope).

Scientists cannot yet explain whether the amyloid plaques cause Alzheimer's disease or if they are a byproduct of the disease. However, what is known is that the abnormal processing of the APP appears to be a key component in the development of Alzheimer's disease. This is why an enormous amount of effort is being put into studying the nature of amyloid plaques: How is it toxic to neurons? How are plaques formed and deposited? How can the number of plaques in the brain be reduced, removed, or prevented from forming? Scientists agree that understanding the function of APP and being able to inhibit or delay its production are keys to unlocking the mystery of Alzheimer's disease.

GENETICS

Generally Alzheimer's disease can be separated into early-onset and late-onset disease. Early onset, the much less common type, is considered strongly genetic, which means that the illness runs in families. Early-onset dementia can start as early as age 30. The more common form, late-onset Alzheimer's disease, usually begins after age 60 and is more likely to be caused by multiple factors, including genetic, environmental, and lifestyle factors.

Genetic studies into early-onset Alzheimer's disease have revealed that there are three chromosomes—chromosomes 21, 14, 1—that play a key role in the illness. Researchers found that families in which early-onset Alzheimer's disease is common have a mutation in selected genes of these chromosomes. On chromosome 21, the mutation causes the production of an abnormal amyloid precursor protein (APP). On chromosome 14, the mutation produces an abnormal protein called presenilin 1, and on chromosome 1, the mutation produces a protein called presenilin 2. Studies have shown that if just one of these inherited genes contains a mutation, it can lead to the development of early-onset Alzheimer's disease.[24]

These findings have strengthened the so-called amyloid hypothesis because they suggest that mutations in amyloid precursor protein (APP) are indeed related to Alzheimer's disease, making chromosome 21 a particular risk factor for the development of Alzheimer's disease. The role of presenilins 1 and 2 remains unclear. Some scientists have suggested that presenilin may be one of the enzymes that clips APP to form the beta-amyloid fragments known to form the amyloid plaques.[24]

Scientists have studied identical twins and noticed a genetic component relating to late-onset dementia. If one of the twins has Alzheimer's disease, then approximately 40 percent of the co-twins also develop it.[36] However, there is usually a long delay before the onset of Alzheimer's disease in the second twin, which suggests that environmental factors, not just genetic factors, contribute to the development of the illness.[37]

Another fact supporting genetic risk factors for Alzheimer's disease is seen in patients with Down's syndrome. Those who live beyond age 40 develop amyloid plaques in their cortex and Alzheimer's-like symptoms. Down's syndrome is caused by an extra chromosome 21, the same chromosome that scientists have identified as a risk factor for Alzheimer's disease.[38]

In addition, scientists have noticed that chromosome 19 is somehow related to late-onset Alzheimer's disease. They found that a protein called apolipoprotein E (ApoE), a product of a gene found on chromosome 19, binds quickly and tightly to beta-amyloid, making it more stable and more likely to become

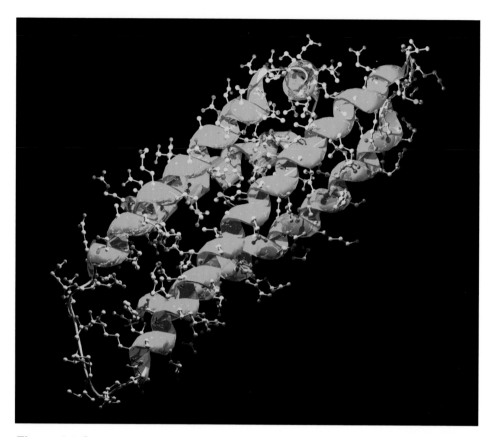

Figure 6.1 Computer model of an apolipoprotein E (ApoE) molecule. One form of the gene that makes ApoE increases the risk of developing Alzheimer's disease. © *Alfred Pasieka/Photo Researchers, Inc.*

a part of the amyloid plaque, thus increasing the risk of AD.[24] This has led scientists to suggest that one form of this gene on chromosome 19 may be a risk factor for late-onset Alzheimer's disease. We all have ApoE in our systems, since its major function is to help carry cholesterol in the body. In general, however, current research seems to support the idea that causes for the late-onset Alzheimer's disease are more likely to be triggered by a combination of environmental or lifestyle factors and genetic factors.

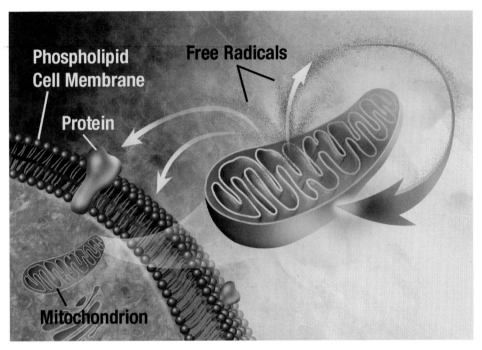

Figure 6.2 Oxygen free radicals seen here damaging the mitochondrion of a cell can destroy or damage neurons over time. © *Alzheimer's Disease Education and Referral Center, a service of the National Institute on Aging*

OXIDATIVE STRESS

Another factor that might play a role in the development of Alzheimer's disease is oxidative stress. Damage from a type of molecule called **oxygen free radicals** can destroy or damage neurons over time, leading to a loss of function. It is believed that free radicals help cells fight infection, but they can also damage nearby molecules like proteins, lipids, and nucleic acids in the cell if they are present in abnormally high concentrations. Cellular damage caused by free radicals can then set off a vicious cycle that produces more free radicals. This cycle is called oxidative damage. Some scientists believe that providing the body with supplementary antioxidants like vitamin E can protect against oxidative damage and Alzheimer's disease.[24, 39]

NEUROFIBRILLARY TANGLES

The neurofibrillary tangles seen in Alzheimer's disease are a significant characteristic of the disease. As discussed above and in Chapter 4, both amyloid plaques and neurofibrillary tangles are present in the brains of people who have died of Alzheimer's disease. It is not clear if the neurofibrillary tangles by themselves in the brain can cause dementia or if amyloid plaques also need to be present to cause disease. Neurofibrillary tangles are a visible knot of microtubules. Microtubules are part of the neuron's skeleton that normally help uphold the structure of the cell and keep the neuron healthy by transporting nutrients and facilitating communication within the neuron. The microtubules are supported by the tau protein. When the tau protein is abnormal or not able to support the microtubules, the microtubules collapse and form neurofibrillary tangles. Tangles prevent transportation of nutrients and communication within the neuron, and the neuron may die. Scientists believe that the tau protein is chemically changed in Alzheimer's disease. The abnormal tau protein is associated with other diseases as well. There is a group of dementias called **tauopathies** that have in common abnormalities with the tau protein. These illnesses include frontotemporal dementia, which destroys brain cells in the frontal and temporal areas of the brain (see Chapter 5). Symptoms of these tauopathies include changes in personality, social behavior, and language ability, difficulties in thinking and decision-making, poor coordination and balance, psychiatric symptoms, and dementia. Scientists have developed several mouse models that produce neurofibrillary tangles with a faulty tau protein. These mice are genetically programmed to produce neurofibrillary tangles in the brain. This mice model is helping scientists understand what role the tau protein might play in Alzheimer's dementia and other tauopathies.[24, 39]

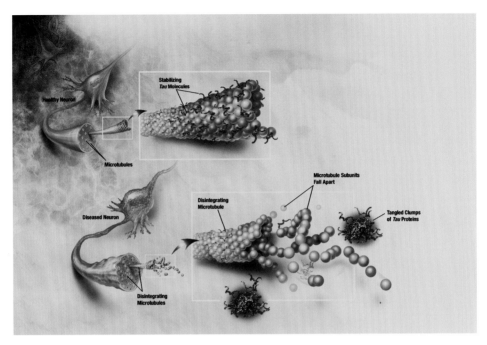

Figure 6.3 In healthy neurons, tau proteins support microtubule structures, but in diseased neurons, the support structure crumbles, releasing tau proteins that form neurofibrillary tangles. © *Alzheimer's Disease Education and Referral Center, a service of the National Institute on Aging*

INFLAMMATION

Some scientists believe that inflammation in the brain may cause Alzheimer's disease. Yet inflammation is a way the body's immune system tries to fight injury or disease. Signs of inflammation are redness, swelling, pain, or fever. During inflammation, specific cells and compounds called **microglia** are activated, which then activate other compounds that cause the inflammation. Their job is to get rid of dead cells and other waste products in the brain.

The fact that microglia cells are present in the plaques found in the brains of patients with Alzheimer's disease makes scientists think there may be links between microglia activity and the symptoms of Alzheimer's disease. Studies have shown that

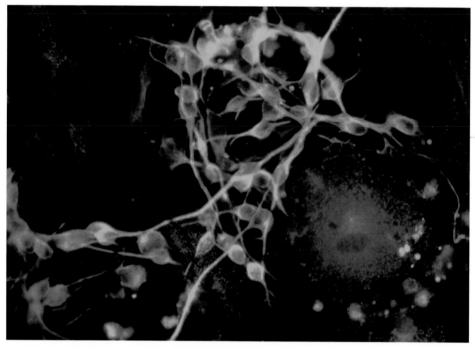

Figure 6.4 The large cell stained red at the lower right is a microglia. The green strands at the center are a tangle of neuron cells interconnected with neuron fibers. © Nancy Kedersha/UCLA/Photo Researchers, Inc.

people who have been taking large doses of nonsteroidal **anti-inflammatory drugs** (NSAIDs) have a lower likelihood of developing Alzheimer's disease. The data are still inconclusive. Some suggest that long-term use of NSAIDs—over a period of several years—may have a protective effect whereas other studies of one year's use have not shown any benefits from NSAIDs. Scientists have not yet determined if inflammation is harmful or beneficial for the brain. Several studies support the idea that inflammation is harmful, because it starts a chain reaction that cause damage and death to neurons and perhaps lead to the formation of the amyloid plaques. Other studies support the idea that some aspects of inflammation are helpful in healing the brain and reducing the number of plaques.[24, 26, 39, 40, 41]

LIFESTYLE

Since vascular dementia is caused by strokes, preventing strokes is the most important aspect of treatment and causative studies. Once brain damage has occurred, no treatment can reverse it. However, future strokes can be prevented by treating the risk factors from stroke. High blood pressure is a major risk factor for stroke and it can be treated with medication and lifestyle changes. Diabetes and high cholesterol are other risk factors that can similarly be treated. In addition to prescribing medications for these conditions, doctors routinely provide advice about healthy lifestyles, including regular exercise, avoiding smoking and excess alcohol, and eating a low-fat diet.

Medications like aspirin or warfarin, a blood-thinning medication, are sometimes prescribed to prevent blood clots. If the blood vessels have already narrowed, doctors may also recommend surgical procedures such as carotid endarterectomy, angioplasty, or stenting. These are surgical procedures that doctors use to try to counteract or widen the narrowing of the blood vessels.

DEMENTIA DUE TO PARKINSON'S DISEASE

The causes of dementia due to Parkinson's disease (DPD) are unclear. Parkinson's disease is a progressive brain disorder that mainly causes problems in movement, such as tremors and stiffness of the limbs. It appears to be caused by a deficiency in the neurotransmitter dopamine in the brain region called the basal ganglia. Approximately 20 percent of patients with Parkinson's disease also develop dementia. Some studies have suggested that patients with DPD have changes in the parietal and temporal regions of their cerebral cortex similar to those seen in Alzheimer's disease. It has been suggested that DPD could be due to the simultaneous occurrence of Alzheimer's disease in the same patient. Indeed, autopsies of some patients who died of Parkinson's disease with dementia show very similar changes in their brains to those seen in Alzheimer's disease, such as plaques and tangles. Scientists do not think that the dementia is due to the pronounced dopamine deficiency that causes the motor problems.

TREATMENTS OF DEMENTIA

The first and most important step in the treatment of any dementia is to identify any other illnesses that may be contributing to or causing the symptoms and treat them accordingly. As discussed earlier, some medical conditions may have dementia-like symptoms but, on closer examination, another condition is responsible.

Currently there is no cure for any form of dementia. However, there are medications that can be used to improve some symptoms and improve the quality of life of people who suffer from dementias. Treatment approaches for dementias are always multifaceted. When doctors decide what treatment to recommend, they have to think about several different factors. They need to consider whether medications might be helpful, or whether the possible benefits outweigh the risks of side effects from the medication. They also need to decide whether cognitive enhancers (related to thinking or reasoning) are needed, and which specific symptoms should be treated. They also need to assess if behavioral strategies need to be implemented and how to mobilize family support.

Medications

Medications are usually used either to treat the cognitive symptoms or behavioral symptoms of dementia. Most pharmacological agents used in treatment of cognitive symptoms of dementia increase the levels of the neurotransmitter acetylcholine in the brain. This chemical messenger exists both in the **peripheral**

nervous system and the **central nervous system**. In the peripheral nervous system, acetylcholine controls muscle contractions and hormone secretion. In the brain, this neurotransmitter is important for memory functioning and thinking. The drugs used to treat Alzheimer's disease are called **cholinesterase inhibitors**. They are currently the most commonly prescribed medications for Alzheimer's dementia. These drugs are believed to act by raising the levels of brain acetylcholine by inhibiting the enzyme cholinesterase. Medications that act thorough these mechanisms include donezepil (Aricept®), rivastigmine (Exelon®), galantamine (Reminyl®), and tetrahydroaminoacridine (tacrine, Cognex®). All these medications seem to produce a slight improvement in cognitive functioning in patients with mild to moderate dementia but do not have an effect on severe dementia.[42] These medications seem to be similarly effective, varying mainly in their side effects. Side effects include nausea, diarrhea, insomnia, fatigue, muscle cramps, and anorexia but do not affect every person in the same way or to the same degree; also, patients often better tolerate a medication after a few weeks.[42]

A new type of medication for the treatment of Alzheimer's disease targets their effect on altering the function of the neurotransmitter **glutamate** in the brain. This neurotransmitter is important for learning and memory, but too much of it can be toxic and damage neurons. The first drug in this class is called memantine (Namenda®). It regulates glutamate by blocking one type of glutamate receptor.

Treating underlying depression, which can mimic dementia or make its symptoms much worse, is crucial. There are several different antidepressants that can be used for this purpose. Sometimes psychotherapy, or talk therapy, is used along with the medication treatment. There are different groups of antidepressant medications. The SSRIs, or selective serotonin reuptake inhibitors—for example, sertraline (Zoloft®), fluoxetine (Prozac®), paroxetine (Paxil®), or escitalopram (Lexapro®)—are most often used. Anxiety can be treated with antidepressants, a medicine called buspirone (BuSpar®), or benzodiazepines, such as clonazepam (Klonopin®).

Patients with moderate to severe dementia often have symptoms of agitation, **paranoid** ideations (suspicious thoughts), hallucinations, delusions (fixed false beliefs), physical aggression, and wandering. These symptoms may become major problems at home, as well as in nursing homes or hospitals. Many medications can be used to treat these symptoms, including antipsychotic drugs. The newer forms, the so-called atypical antipsychotics drugs like risperidone (Risperdal®), olanzapine (Zyprexa®), and quiatepine (Seroquel®), may be very helpful in controlling agitation and psychosis associated with dementia. Physical aggression can be treated with either antipsychotic drugs or medications like carbamazepine (Tegretol®) or valproic acid (Depakote®). Many of these medications have serious side effects, so the prescribing doctor must weigh the risks and benefits before prescribing them. No medications are risk free, and they should only be prescribed by a specialist. In 2005, researchers found that using antipsychotics in treatment of patients with dementias increases their risk of strokes and sudden death.

A patient with dementia and serious medical problems presents a big challenge. Patients with advanced dementia are unable to express their distress verbally and may be unable to communicate their pain and discomfort. A headache, toothache from a cavity, constipation, and other minor pains can develop into more serious conditions. A patient's agitation may be an expression of pain, depression, or anxiety, or be an unexplained part of the illness itself.

Behavioral Approach

When people start to lose cognitive functions, they become much more sensitive to their surroundings. Patients with dementia do best with optimal stimulation. Understimulation, for example, limiting patients in their activities and routines, may cause withdrawal and even depression. Overstimulation, with too many activities, visitors, or loud music or sounds, may cause agitation and confusion. It should be easy to empathize with a confused person with dementia who cannot remember the past, for whom the present is full of new and strange things, and to whom the concept of future is a blur. Forgetting how to use ordinary items like forks and knives and light switches can be very scary and create anxiety or agitation. Family visits may become terrifying events to someone who can no longer remember or recognize their loved ones.

Familiar surroundings help maximize a patient's cognitive functioning. An important part of behavioral treatment strategy is to increase the patient's sense of security and provide him or her with set daily routines. Keeping clocks, calendars, night-lights, checklists, and diaries around the house can help memory. If the patient has to move or stay in a hospital temporarily, it helps to have familiar objects, including photographs of family members and friends, to create a homier atmosphere. Newspapers, radio, and television often help maintain awareness and contact with the world outside.

Practical approaches, such as anticipating potential sources of agitation and then eliminating or changing them, can make a big difference in avoiding angry outbursts or agitation. If seeing objects that the patient has lost the ability to use causes rage, those objects should be removed from the patient's vicinity, if possible. A behavioral specialist, psychologist, geriatric nurse, or psychiatrist can help assess the home and suggest changes in the surroundings to minimize anxiety, agitation, and behavioral disturbances. In this way, less medication may be needed to control outbursts or unwanted behavior.

FAMILY SUPPORT

Family members care for a large number of patients with dementia at home. Most often spouses take on the role of the primary caretaker, followed by children and grandchildren.[24]

Family members who care for their loved ones with Alzheimer's disease are at high risk for developing depression or exhaustion.[13] Education and counseling about the nature of the illness can help caregivers cope with the everyday frustrations common to people with Alzheimer's disease. Caregivers need the ability to reflect on any feelings of anger and confusion that frequently result from the patient's behavior.

Finding ways to help families cope with loved ones suffering from dementia is a relatively new area of research and clinical approaches. Studies have resulted in more information about the kinds of support that are best for caregivers. For example, the traditional method of a caregivers' support group, while enormously helpful to participants, is not always practical for everyone. Taking time away from a loved one with dementia requires another person to oversee care. For these reasons, a project called the Alzheimer's Disease Support Center was started in 1989.[24] It is a website that provides expert medical advice, information about the latest research, and has a component allowing people to share thoughts and feelings by posting messages online. The web site allows access 24 hours a day, seven days a week at http://adsc.ohioalzcenter.org/.

Outlook
for the Future

Most research into the treatment of dementias is focused on trying to understand the disease process. As more is known about the disease process, more treatments can be developed to prevent, delay, and, ultimately, cure dementias. Some current research focuses on preventing or delaying the formation of the amyloid plaques. Other studies are looking for ways to boost the body's immune system to stop the production of the plaques. Although dementias are currently incurable, it is important to remember that they are not untreatable. One of the most appealing treatment approaches is to target the amyloid plaque and try to prevent its formation, or try to remove it once it has emerged. There are currently several treatment strategies under investigation.

STUDIES IN MICE LEAD TO HUMAN STUDIES FOR A VACCINE

The development of transgenic mice has become an effective way to study and try to cure dementias and Alzheimer's disease in a laboratory setting. Transgenic mice are mice that have had DNA artificially introduced into one or more of their cells. These mice are thus genetically programmed to develop amyloid plaques. Some mice were developed to produce both plaques and tangles, making them even more useful for Alzheimer's research.[44] Researchers noticed in 1999 that a vaccine called AN-1792, created to stimulate the immune system to

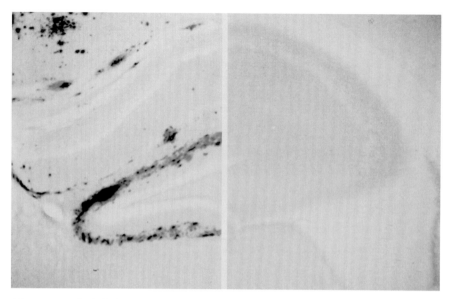

Figure 7.1 At left is brain tissue from a mouse genetically engineered to produce the dark protein deposits characteristic of Alzheimer's disease. Opposite is brain tissue from a similar mouse of the same age treated with an experimental anti-Alzheimer's vaccine. © AP Images

attack plaques, prevented plaque formation in these mice when they were vaccinated at an early age. In addition, it seemed that if older mice with already developed plaques were given the vaccine, their number of plaques was reduced. Researchers hypothesized that the vaccine triggered the immune system to start removing plaques or prevent them from developing.[45] These initial findings led to tests of the vaccine on human volunteers but the vaccine was not well tolerated. Despite this apparent failure, important data were gathered. For example, about 20 percent of those people who received the vaccine developed high levels of **antibodies** to beta-amyloid plaques. An antibody is a specific protein produced by the body that can attack and or kill foreign particles in the body such as bacteria or a plaque. Those volunteers who developed the highest numbers of antibodies declined the least in their average performance on mental functioning tests.

Brain autopsies of some volunteers' unrelated deaths showed lower than expected numbers of plaques.

CAN ANTI-INFLAMMATORY DRUGS PREVENT OR SLOW ALZHEIMER'S DISEASE?

Many scientists are looking at anti-inflammatory medications, because of findings that show signs of inflammation in the brains of people suffering from Alzheimer's disease. Inflammation is a normal protective reaction of the body, but if it lasts too long, it can cause damage to body tissue. Some large observational studies point to the fact that people who took large doses of nonsteroidal anti-inflammatory drugs (NSAIDs) have a reduced likelihood of developing Alzheimer's disease. NSAIDs include aspirin and aspirin-like compounds that are used to treat pain, inflammation, and fever. To date, results from larger studies have been inconclusive, in part because NSAIDs, have some adverse effects like other medications. Side effects from NSAIDs include dizziness, fatigue, and high blood pressure, although not everyone gets them. Nevertheless, there are still several ongoing studies trying to understand the initial positive outcome of NSAID trials because it is not clear if NSAIDs can help prevent dementia and, if so, which one of the many NSAIDs available would be most promising.

CAN ANTI-CHOLESTEROL DRUGS PREVENT DEMENTIA?

Several studies have shown that people with cardiovascular risk factors, including high cholesterol, have an increased risk of developing Alzheimer's disease or vascular dementia. Statins are drugs that reduce cholesterol levels in the blood. Some research studies have found a positive link between taking a cholesterol-reducing drug and a decreased risk of developing Alzheimer's disease. However, as with the studies on NSAIDs, some studies have not supported this notion.

In chapter 6 we discussed chromosome 19, which is responsible for producing the cholesterol-carrying protein ApoE. ApoE is a protein that we all have, and one variation, the ApoE e4, has been shown to promote the production of the amyloid plaques, which is the hallmark for Alzheimer's disease, and is thus considered to be a risk factor for Alzheimer's disease. However, there is not yet enough evidence to support the use of statins to prevent Alzheimer's disease. Large clinical trials will be required to clarify this hypothesis. Also, it is not clear how the statins modify the process of Alzheimer's disease.[46]

WHAT ABOUT ANTIOXIDANTS?

The interest in using antioxidants for treatment of dementia comes from the idea that **oxygen free radicals** can cause damage to neurons in the brain and thus cause dementia symptoms. **Antioxidants** like vitamin E or selegiline (an antioxidant drug used to treat Parkinson's disease) defend the cells from the damaging attacks of free radicals. A 1997 research study supported the use of antioxidants vitamin E and seleginile to delay the progress from moderate to severe dementia, including institutionalization and death. However, the drugs were not shown to have a definitive effect on memory and thinking.[39] Again, the results are promising but inconclusive. Further studies are needed to clarify the possible benefits of antioxidants.

WHAT ABOUT NERVE GROWTH FACTORS?

A very innovative approach to the treatment of Alzheimer's disease is sought in studies of **nerve growth factors**. Nerve growth factors are proteins produced by the neuron involved in regulating nerve maturation in early prenatal stages and are very important in cell survival, repair, and regeneration later in life. Because of their significance in the survival of neurons, they have attracted interest from researchers who study Alzheimer's disease and other neurodegenerative diseases.

The practical problem in using these proteins is that they are so large that they cannot easily reach the brain tissue. Currently researchers are working to develop smaller compounds that can reach the brain and mimic the effects of nerve growth factors. A compound called leteprinim can reach brain tissue and activates genes that produce nerve growth factors. In preclinical animal studies, leteprinim showed improvement in the memories of old and young mice. It was also initially found to be safe in humans in small clinical trials in 2001. However, in larger clinical trials, even when it showed some benefits to some individuals with Alzheimer's disease, it didn't show greater overall benefits than treatment with an inactive substance. These results were published in 2002. The compound has been withdrawn from further studies, but it is still of interest for Alzheimer's disease research and more studies are needed.[39, 47]

ADDITIONAL DRUGS IN DEVELOPMENT

Two other treatments for the cognitive symptoms of Alzheimer's disease are currently in early clinical trials and considered promising. One of them, the compound CX516 (Ampalex™), acts by regulating the levels of the neurotransmitter glutamate, which plays an important role in memory and learning. It works through a specific glutamate receptor called **AMPA** ($\propto$-Amino-3-hydroxy-5-methylisoxazole-4-propionic acid receptor). So far, early clinical trials have shown the drug to be safe and well tolerated. Further trials are needed to determine its safety and effectiveness.

Another drug, MKC-231, was developed to activate the acetylcholine system. The currently available cognitive enhancers increase the levels of acetylcholine in the brain by inhibiting its breakdown by the enzyme acetylcholinesterase.

MKC-231 is believed to make more choline available. Choline is the raw material for the production of acetylcholine. This drug is currently being tested for safety and effectiveness.

CAN DEMENTIAS BE PREVENTED?

There is not yet a cure but there are treatments for symptoms. Many scientists are studying ways to prevent the development of the diseases altogether. Right now scientists are able to identify people at high risk of developing dementia. This can be a challenging task, but by using brain imaging to identify any abnormalities, through structural interviews about lifestyle and medical history, and neuropsychological tests to look for personality traits, scientists try to identify people at high risk for developing dementia. For example, scientists are closely tracking people with Mild Cognitive Impairment (MCI), which may be a preclinical phase for Alzheimer's disease, for clues on why some go on to develop dementia and others do not.

Many large population studies have tried to focus on factors in people's lifestyle and environment to identify those who are more likely to develop dementias. Even with a genetic predisposition for late-onset dementia, research has suggested that efforts to delay the onset and the progress of dementias might be possible. For example, research has suggested that staying in good physical health, keeping your brain active and eating a healthy diet can help prevent dementias. One such large-scale research study is the Nun Study, or the Religious Orders Study.[23]

THE NUN STUDY

Studying people over time who live similar lifestyles with similar daily activities and environments provides important information about an illness. These kinds of studies help scientists identify possible preventive factors. In studies conducted by the National Institute of Aging called the Religious Orders Study or

Slowing the onset of Alzheimer's

Little is known about how and why Alzheimer's happens, but research indicates that there may be effective ways to prevent it or at least slow its progress.

A degenerative pattern

Alzheimer's works fast, reducing neuro-function significantly in just a few years. Positron Emission Tomography (PET) imagery, by measuring brain activity, has helped doctors reveal the areas of the brain most affected.

Normal brain - Red areas are highest in neuro-activity.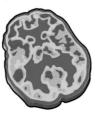

Alzheimer's afflicted brain - Eight years later, function is reduced by almost a third.

Getting a head start

Although there is little definitive research, a few theories on preventative measures are peaking interest:

 Estrogen and ginkgo biloba - Studies are underway that may link these substances to Alzheimer's prevention, possibly due to anti-inflammatory or circulatory properties.

 Anti-inflammatory drugs - Animal studies show these drugs can limit the production of amyloid, the protein deposits that are characteristic of an Alzheimer's afflicted brain.

 Statin drugs - Originally prescribed for high cholesterol, doctors observed that the drugs reduced Alzheimer's risk as well, leading many to draw a correlation between cholesterol levels and Alzheimer's disease.

 Folate - High levels of the amino acid homocysteine have been shown to increase risk of Alzheimer's and heart disease. The nutrient folate, already added to flour, is known to lower it.

 Mental exercise - Some believe that getting lots of mental activity can make the brain stronger and more equipped to function even if Alzheimer's attacks.

SOURCES: UCLA, David Geffen School of Medicine; Associated Press   **AP**

Figure 7.2 © *AP Images*

the Nun Study, the mental and physical capacities of 678 older nuns in the Roman Catholic order School Sisters of Notre Dame were investigated. Participants underwent annual detailed physical and mental exams and agreed to donate their brains for scientific research after they died. For decades their lifestyles and daily activities were closely monitored and compared to their cognitive test scores and, ultimately, to the findings after death from their brains. These studies have produced large databases of information that can be examined as scientists continue to learn more about the disease.

Some interesting results have come from these studies already. For example, researchers found that the risk for developing Alzheimer's disease was 47 percent lower in people who were involved in seven mentally stimulating activities daily. These activities included reading, playing cards or other games, or going to museums. It has been suggested that these activities somehow protect the brain from dementia-associated damages. Another interesting finding from the study was that there was a relationship between the richness in language and ideas and complex usage of grammar seen in the participants' diaries written in their youths and the lower number of signs of Alzheimer's disease in the participants' brains after death. Those nuns whose brains showed the most signs of Alzheimer's disease also had low grammatical complexity and idea density in their written autobiographies. The results from this and other studies have led to further support of the hypothesis "Use-it-or-lose-it" for brainpower.[23, 24]

WHAT CAN YOU DO?

The Greek proverb *Mens sana in corpore sano*, or "Healthy mind in healthy body," still holds true today when it comes to many degenerative brain disorders. The best way to prevent Alzheimer's disease or other dementias is to take good care of

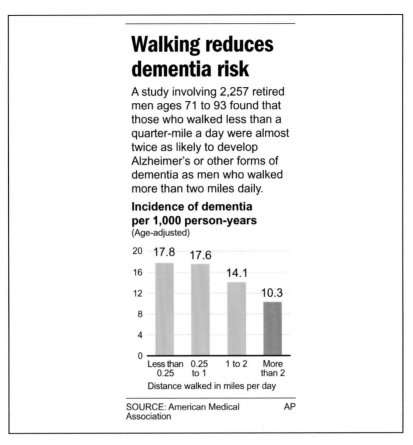

Figure 7.3 © *AP Images*

your overall health. Make sure you eat a balanced diet, with multiple sources of energy and fibers from fruits and vegetables. Avoid high-fat, high-salt foods and excessive amounts of alcohol. Exercise regularly, avoid stress, and make sure you get enough sleep. All of this will protect your general health. These measures are known to be an important part of preventing cardiovascular diseases. High blood pressure, high cholesterol, and a sedentary lifestyle are factors known to increase the risk of a cardiovascular incident, such as a stroke, which is a leading cause of vascular dementia. So you can see that keeping your body healthy keeps your brain healthy.[48]

Staying mentally active all of your life is important. Brain-stimulating activities like reading, solving crossword puzzles, learning new facts and ideas, and maintaining skills you have already achieved are all important ways to delay, if not to avoid, the illness of dementia.

Avoiding stress—especially chronic stress—is important. It has been shown that in older people chronic stress may cause depression or anxiety, which can cause poor memory and concentration.[49]

Staying socially active by connecting with other people will help keep your mind agile. Throughout your life, spend time with friends, join a club, or take continuing education courses.

Living safely, for example, by wearing a helmet while biking to avoid head injury, is important for the prevention of traumatic brain injuries and irreversible brain damage.

While the prognosis for dementia is grim because it remains an incurable disease, with healthy living and high activity levels an individual can reduce the odds of getting this devastating disease. Also, the overall consensus among scientists is that viable treatments for dementias exist today, and advanced treatments, if not a cure, can be achieved in the foreseeable future through research.

1. Spitzer, Robert L. et al., eds. *DSM-IV Case Book*. Washington, D.C.: American Psychiatric Press, 1994.
2. Malmgren, Roberta, "Epidemiology of Aging," in *Textbook of Geriatric Neuropsychiatry*, eds. C. Edward Coffey and Jeffrey Cummings. (Washington, D.C.: American Psychiatric Press, 2000) 57.
3. Kaplan, Harold I., and Benjamin J. Saddock. *Synopsis of Psychiatry; Behavioral Sciences/Clinical Psychiatry*, 8th ed. Baltimore, Md.: Lippincott Williams & Wilkins, 1998.
4. Hebert, Liesi E. et al., "Alzheimer Disease in the US Population, Prevalence Estimates Using the 2000 Census," *Archives in Neurology* 60 (Aug 2003): 1119–1122.
5. Evans, Denis A. et al., "Prevalence of Alzheimer's in a Community Population of Older Persons," *Journal of American Medical Association*, 262, no. 18 (1989): 2551–2556.
6. U.S. Congress Office of Technology Assessment, *Losing a Million Minds: Confronting the Tragedy of Alzheimer's Disease and Other Dementias*. U.S. Congress Office of Technology Assessment: U.S. Government Printing Office, 1987.
7. Turner, Scott, "Neurologic Aspects of Alzheimer's Disease" in *Handbook of Dementia*, eds. Peter Lichtenberg, Daniel L. Murman, and Alan M. Mellow (Hoboken, N.J.: Wiley and Sons, 2003): 1–21.
8. Arehart-Treichel, Joan, "Age of Alzheimer's Onset in Latinos Puzzles Scientists," *Psychiatric News* (October 1, 2004): 34.
9. Roman, Gustavo, "Neurologic, Aspects of Vascular Dementia: Basic Concepts, Diagnosis, and Management" in *Handbook of Dementia*, eds. Peter Lichtneberg, Daniel L. Murman, and Alan M. Mellow (Hoboken, N.J.: Wiley and Sons, 2003): 149–165.
10. Caine Eric D., Hillel Grossman, and Jeffrey M.,Lyness, "Delirium, Dementia, and Amnestic and Other Cognitive Disorders and Mental Disorders due to a General Medical Condition" in *Comprehensive Textbook of Psychiatry*, eds. Harold I. Kaplan and, Benjamin J. Saddock 6th ed. (Baltimore Md.: Williams and Wilkins, 1997): 733.
11. Kaufman, David Mylan, "Dementia" in *Clinical Neurology for Psychiatrists*, ed. David Mylan Kaufman. (Philadelphia, Penn.: W.B.Saunders, 2001): 127.
12. Kaufman, David Mylan,"Dementia" in *Clinical Neurology for Psychiatrists*ed. David Mylan Kaufman. (Philadelphia, Penn.: W.B.Saunders, 2001): 369.
13. Neundorfer, Marcia M. et al., "A Longitudinal Study of the Relationship Between Levels of Depression Among Persons with Alzheimer's Disease and Levels of Depression Among Their Family Caregivers," *The Journals of Gerontology, Series B, Psychological Sciences and Social Sciences* 56, no. 5 (2001): 301–313.
14. National Institute of Aging; National Institutes of Health (NIH), *2001–2002 Alzheimer's Disease Progress Report,* NIH Publication No. 03–5333 (July 2003): 2.
15. Ernst, Richard L., Hay, Joel W. "The U.S. Economic and Social Costs of Alzheimer's Disease Revisited," *American Journal of Public Health* 84, no. 8 (1994): 1261–1264. (Note: This study cites 1991 data, which were updated to 1994 figures in the *American Journal of Public Health*'s 1994 press release. This article is cited in the National Institutes of Health (NIH) publication *2001–2002 Alzheimer's Disease Progress Report,* NIH Publication No. 03–5333 (July 2003): 2.)

16. Rice, Dorothy P. et al., "The Economic
    Burden of Alzheimer's Disease," *Health
    Affairs* 12, no. 2 (Summer 1993):
    164–176.
17. Alzheimer's Association. URL:
    http://www.alz.org.resources/topicIndex.
    Downloaded April 14, 2006.
18. Medina, John, *What You Need to Know
    About Alzheimer's*. Oakland, Calif.: New
    Harbinger Publications, Inc., 1999.
19. Small, Gary W., *Alzheimer's disease and
    other dementias* in *Comprehensive
    Textbook of Psychiatry*, eds. Harold I.
    Kaplan and Benjamin J. Saddock.7th ed.
    (Philadelphia, Penn.: Lippincott Williams
    & Wilkins, 2000): 3068.
20. Kaplan, Harold I., and Benjamin J.
    Saddock, *Synopsis of Psychiatry;
    Behavioral Sciences/Clinical Psychiatry*,
    8th ed. (Baltimore, Md.: Lippincott
    Williams & Wilkins, 1998): 56.
21. Neuroscience Resources for Kids. URL:
    http//:staff.washington.edu/
    chudler/aging.html. Updated April 4,
    2006.
22. Boone, Kyle Brauer, "Neuropsychological
    Evaluation" in *Comprehensive Textbook of
    Psychiatry*, eds. Harold I. Kaplan and
    Benjamin J.Saddock. 7th ed.
    (Philadelphia, Penn.: Lippincott Williams
    & Wilkins, 2000): 3027–3033.
23. Snowdon, David A. et al., "Linguistic
    Ability Early in Life and Cognitive
    Function and Alzheimer's Disease in Late
    Life: Findings from the Nun Study,"
    Journal of American Medical Association
    275 (February 21, 1996): 528–532.
24. National Institute of Aging and National
    Institutes of Health (NIH), *Alzheimer's
    Disease: Unraveling the Mystery*, NIH
    Publication No. 02–3782 (December
    2003): 20.
25. Paganini-Hill, Annlia, Henderson,
    Victoria W., "Estrogen Deficiency and
    Risk of Alzheimer's Disease in Women,"

American Journal of Epidemiology 140,
    no. 3 (1994): 256–261.
26. Stewart, Walter F. et al., "Risk of
    Alzheimer's Disease and Duration of
    NSAID Use," *Neurology* 48 (1997):
    626–632.
27. Graves, Amy B. et al., "The Association
    Between Head Trauma and Alzheimer's
    Disease," *American Journal of
    Epidemiology* 131 (1990): 491–501.
28. U.S. Department of Health and Human
    Services, Public Health Services; National
    Institutes of Health (NIH); National
    Institute of Aging, *Fact Sheet*, NIH
    Publication No. 02–3433 (July 2003).
29. Reichman, William E., "Nondegenerative
    Dementing Disorder" in *Textbook of
    Geriatric Neuropsychiatry*, eds., C.
    Edward Coffey and Jeffrey L. Cummings.
    (Washington, D.C.: American Psychiatric
    Press, 2000): 491–509.
30. Helpguide. URL
    http//:www.helpguide.org/elder/lewy
    body_disease. Downloaded on April 14,
    2006.
31. Lerner, Alan J., and Peter J. Whitehouse,
    "Neuropsychiatric Aspects of Dementias
    Associated with Motor Dysfunction" in
    *Textbook of Neuropsychiatry and Clinical
    Neurosciences*, eds., Stuart C. Yudofsky,
    and Robert E. Hales. (Washington D.C.:
    American Psychiatric Publishing, Inc.,
    2002): 937.
32. Alzheimer's Disease Education and
    Referral (ADERA) Center, *Connections* 9
    (2002).
33. Podell, Kenneth, and Mark R. Lovell,
    Neuropscychological Assessment in
    Textbook of Geriatric Neuropsychiatry,
    eds. C. Edward Coffey and Jeffrey L.
    Cummings. (Washington, D.C.:
    American Psychiatric Press, 2000):
    143–164.
34. Reiman, Eric M., "Neuroimaging:
    Overview" in *Comprehensive Textbook of*

Psychiatry, eds. Harold I. Kaplan and Benjamin J. Saddock. 7th ed., (Lippincott Williams & Wilkins, Philadelphia, Penn., 2000): 3038.

35. Jackson, George R. andAnthony E. Lang, "Hyperkinetic Movement Disorders" in *Textbook of Geriatric Neuropsychiatry*, eds. C. Edward Coffey and Jeffrey L. Cummings. (Washington, D.C.: American Psychiatric Press, 2000): 531–557.

36. Gatz, Margaret et al., "Heritability for Alzheimer's Disease: The Study of Dementia in Swedish Twins," *Journal of Gerontology* 52A (1997): M117–M125.

37. Creasey, H. et al., "Monozygotic Twins Discordant for Alzheimer's Dsease," *Neurology* 39 (1989): 1474–1476.

38. Miller, Bruce L. and Andrew Gustavson, "Alzheimer's Disease and Frontotemporal Dementia" in *Textbook of Geriatric Neuropsychiatry*, eds. C. Edward Coffey and Jeffrey L. Cummings. (Washington, D.C.: American Psychiatric Press, 2000): 511–529.

39. Petersen, R., ed., *Mayo Clinic on Alzheimer's Disease*, New York: Kensington Publishing Corporation, 2002.

40. Launer, Lenore J., "Nonsteroidal Anti-inflammatory Drugs and Alzheimer Disease," *Journal of American Medical Association* 289, no. 21 (June 4, 2001): 2865–2867.

41. int'Veld, Bas A. et al., "Nonsteroidal Anti-inflammatory Drugs and the Risk of Alzheimer's Disease," *New England Journal of Medicine* 345 (Nov. 22, 2001): 1515–1521.

42. Greenberg, Steven M. et al., "Donepezil Therapy in Clinical Practice," *Archives in Neurology* 57 (2000): 94–99.

43. Schatzberg, Alan. F., Jonathan.O. Cole, and Charles DeBattista, *Manual of Clinical Psychopharmacology*, 4th ed., Washington D.C.: American Psychiatric Publishing, Inc., 2005.

44. Lewis, Jada et al., "Enhanced Neurofibrillary Degeneration in Transgenic Mice Expressing Mutant Tau and APP," *Science* vol. 293, no. 5534 (2001): 1487–1491.

45. Vehmas, Anne K. et al "?-Amyloid Peptide Vaccination Results in Marked Changes in Serm and Brain A? Levels in APPswe/PS1?E9 Mice, as Detected by SELDI-TOF-based ProteinChip® Technology," *DNA and Cell Biology* 20 (2001): 713–721.

46. Golde, T.E., "Alzheimer's Disease Therapy: Can the Amyloid Cascade be Halted?" *Journal of Clinical Investigation* 111, no. 1 (2003): 11–18.

47. Wyss-Coray, Tony et al., "TGF-?1 Promotes Microglia Amyloid-? Clearance and Reduces Plaque Burden in Transgenic Mice," *Nature Medicine* 7 (2001): 612–618.

48. Friedland, Robert P. et al., "Patients with Alzheimer's Disease Have Reduced Activities in Midlife Compared with Healthy Control-Group Members," *Proceedings of the National Academy of Science* 98 (2001): 3440–3445.

49. Newcomer, John W. et al., "Decreased Memory Performance in Healthy Humans Induced by Stress-level Cortisol Treatment," *Archives of General Psychiatry* 56 (1999): 527–533.

GLOSSARY

acetylcholine—Main chemical neurotransmitter, or messenger, (neuro-transmitter) in the brain that is important for learning and memory. People with dementia have a shortage of acetylcholine in their brains.

agnosia—Inability to recognize a common object (keys or coins) by touch only.

AMPA receptor—$\propto$-Amino-3-hydroxy-5-methylisoxazole-4-propionic acid receptor. A form of glutamate receptor in the brain.

amnesia—Loss of memory.

amyloid plaques—Insoluble deposits made out of beta-amyloid, a protein fragment cut from Amyloid Precurson Protein found in the space between nerve cells in the brains of people with Alzheimer's dementia.

amyloid precursor protein (APP)—Protein with an unknown function found in the brain. In Alzheimer's disease APP is cut into fragments to form beta-amyloid; where beta-amyloid fragments clump together, amyloid plaques are created.

antibody—Protein produced by the body to attack or kill harmful bacteria or plaque.

anti-inflammatory drug—Drug used to treat pain and swelling.

antioxidants—Substances that inhibit the action of free radicals in the brain, protecting it from damage.

antipsychotic—Medication used to treat psychotic disorders and some-times behavioral problems in dementia patients. Antipsychotics block the action of the neurotransmitter dopamine in the brain.

anxiolytics—Medications used to treat anxiety symptoms, in the drug class called benzodiazepines, or sedatives.

aphasia—Loss of language skills, causing an inability to produce or repeat words or to understand what others are saying.

apolipoprotein E—Protein that transports cholesterol in the body.

apraxia—Inability to perform a movement based on verbal instructions even when nothing is wrong with arms or legs. For example, a patient cannot upon request show how to salute or pretend to comb hair.

atrophy—Condition where cells, including muscle and brain cells, wither, shrink, and ultimately die.

autopsy—Examination of a dead body to try to find out the cause of death.

axons—Part of the neuron that extends out of the cell body and specializes in sending messages to other neurons.

beta-amyloid—Protein fragment of amyloid precursor protein (APP), these clump together to form the amyloid plaques (also called beta-amyloid plaques) found in the space between nerve cells.

bradykinesia—Decrease and slowness in spontaneous movements, especially seen in Parkinson's dementia.

cataracts—Illness of the eye that causes cloudy areas on the lens, damaging vision. Treatable by surgery.

central nervous system—Nerve cells within the brain and spinal cord.

cerebral cortex—Surface layer of the cerebrum (brain) that affects sensory and motor abilities.

cerebrospinal fluid—Liquid that surrounds the brain and spinal cord and fills the four brain ventricles.

cerebrovascular disease—Narrowing of the blood vessels of the brain, increasing risk of stroke and possibly vascular dementia.

cholinesterase inhibitors—Drugs used to treat Alzheimer's disease by affecting levels of acetylcholine in the brain.

chorea—Involuntary, spasmodic movements of arms, legs, and torso. The word *chorea* comes from the Greek word for dance.

chromosomal abnormality—Extra chromosome or a faulty chromosome that can cause an illness or condition. For example, in Down's syndrome a person has an extra chromosome 21, and in Huntington's disease the illness is transmitted by chromosome 4.

clinical syndrome—Medical condition that has a particular group of symptoms.

cognition—Relating to thinking or reasoning.

cortical neurons—Nerve cells found in the part of the brain called the cortex.

CT scan—Computerized tomography, or image displaying cross-sectional views of the body.

delusion—Fixed false belief. For example, people may believe that someone is trying to harm them or that aliens are controlling their behavior.

dementia—Clinical syndrome that impairs memory, thinking, and behavior.

demyelinating disease—Disease that destroys the myelin sheath on nerve cells throughout the body, which causes electric signal transduction to slow.

dopamine—Neurotransmitter in the brain that regulates mood, movement, and cognition.

Down's syndrome—Medical condition caused by an extra chromosome 21. Patients have mental retardation, characteristic facial features, and usually develop Alzheimer's disease if they live beyond age 40.

dura mater—Thick tissue that covers the brain right under the skull.

encephalitis—Infection of the brain.

enzymes—Substances that can cause a chemical reaction or speed one up.

gliosis—Scarring of brain tissue that occurs when nerve cells die.

glutamate—Neurotransmitter in the brain important for learning and memory.

hallucination—Seeing, hearing, or feeling things that do not exist.

hippocampus—Brain structure important for learning, memory and the consolidation of short-term memories to long-term memory.

homocysteine—Blood compound that some scientists have linked with increased risk of developing Alzheimer's disease.

hydrocephalus—Elevated pressure in the fluid that surrounds the brain and the spinal cord. This pressure can prevent the growth of the brain and cause mental retardation. Often results from an unknown injury to the brain.

hyperlipidemia—Elevated levels of cholesterol, or fat cells in the blood.

immune system—System in the body that is activated and defends the body when foreign particles harmful to the body attack it, for example, bacteria or virus.

impaired executive functioning—Disturbances in planning, reasoning, judgment, abstracting, and other intellectual functions.

ischemic heart disease— Narrowing of the blood vessels of the heart, possibly risk factor for dementia.

lability—Instability of mood, or quick shifts from being happy to being sad to being angry.

Lewy bodies—Small protein particles found in various areas of the brain in a sub-type of Alzheimer's disease called Lewy body disease (LBD).

lumbar puncture—Procedure performed by a doctor to extract cerebrospinal fluid with a needle from the lower back.

limbic system—Part of the brain that is the center of emotions and moods.

microglia—Special cells in the immune system that attempt to clear away amyloid plaques from the brains of people with Alzheimer's disease.

MRI scan—Magnetic Resonance Imaging scan, which produces computerized images of internal body tissue.

myelin sheath—Protein that covers the axon of the neuron to help the electrical impulses travel faster.

neoplasia—Abnormal growth of cells that can refer to either harmful growth such as cancer or nonharmful growth.

nerve growth factors—Proteins that promote the growth of nerve cells and may protect some nerve cells from damage.

neurodegenerative—Affecting the nervous system and nerve cells by destroying the nerve cells.

neurofibrillary tangles—Clumps of abnormal tau protein located inside nerve cells in a person with Alzheimer's disease.

neurological—Related to the nervous system.

neuron—Nerve cell in the body.

neurotransmitter—Chemical messenger used by nerve cells to forward information to one another.

oxygen free radicals—Molecule that helps neurons survive by fighting infection, but some scientists believe it can damage neurons if too many are present.

paranoid—Pathologically suspicious.

peripheral nervous system—Nerve cells outside the brain and spinal cord.

presenile dementia—Symptoms of dementia starting earlier than the average age.

presenilin-1 and presenilin-2—Proteins that may be related to the early-onset Alzheimer's disease.

prions—Infectious particles that can cause Creutzfeldt-Jakob disease or mad-cow disease.

progressive—Change that happens gradually.

schizophrenia—Chronic, severe mental illness characterized by hallucinations and delusions, which makes it difficult for patients to relate their thoughts and feelings to the outside world.

secretases—Enzymes that are believed to cut the amyloid precursor protein (APP) into smaller pieces called beta-amyloid; where beta-amyloid fragments clump together, amyloid plaques are created.

sedatives—Medications used to relieve anxiety, often called anxiolytics.

selective serotonine reuptake inhibitors (SSRIs)—Antidepressant medications that increase the amount of the neurotransmitter serotonin in the brain.

senile plaques—See amyloid plaques.

statin—Drug that reduces cholesterol level in the blood.

stroke—Blood clot blocks a blood vessel in the brain, which kills brain cells. Can also be caused by a bleed in the brain with the same result.

sulci—Grooves on the brain.

tau—In a healthy brain, tau is involved in supporting the internal structure of the nerve cell that serves as a transport system for nutrients and other molecules.

tauopathies—Group of dementias that have in common abnormalities of the tau protein.

thalamus—Part of the brain that receives information from the senses and the limbic system.

vacuolisation—Process where holes form in the brain.

Le Vert, Suzanne. *Kaleidoscope: The Brain*. New York: Benchmark Books, 2001.

Mace, Nancy, and Peter V. Rabins. *The 36-Hour Day*. 3d ed. Baltimore, Md.: The Johns Hopkins University Press, 1999.

Petersen, R., ed. *Mayo Clinic on Alzheimer's Disease*. 1st ed. Rochester, Minn.: Mayo Clinic Health Information; New York: Kensington Publishing Corporation, 2002.

Medina, John. *What You Need to Know About Alzheimer's*. 1st ed. Oakland, Calif.: CME, Inc., and New Harbinger Publications, Inc., 1999.

Mumenthaler, Mark, *Neurology*. 2d ed. Stuttgart and New York: Thieme Medical Publishers, 1983.

Willett, Edward. *Alzheimer's Disease*. Berkeley Heights, N.J.: Enslow Publisher, Inc., 2002.

Rosenberg, Roger N., et al. "Translational Research on the Way to Effective Therapy for Alzheimer's Disease," *Archives of General Psychiatry*, 62, no. 11 (November 2005):1186–1192.

Stern, Yaakov, et al. "Influence of Education and Occupation on the Incidence of Alzheimer's Disease," *Journal of American Medical Association*, 271, no. 13 (April 6, 1994):1004–1010.

Yudofsky, Stuart C, and Robert E. Hales. *Textbook of Neuropsychiatry and Clinical Neurosciences*, 4th ed. Washington D.C.: The American Psychiatric Publishing, 2002.

WEB SITES

Alzheimer's Association
http://www.alz.org
Large Web site produced by the premier Alzheimer's disease organization that promotes public awareness, information about treatments, ongoing research, patient-family support, and other subjects.

Alzheimer's Disease Support Center
http://adsc.ohioalzcenter.org
Support Web site provides expert medical advice, information about the latest research, and has a component allowing people to share thoughts and feelings by posting messages online.

Helpguide
http//:helpguide.org/elder/alzheimers_dementian.htm
Expert, non-commercial information on mental health and lifelong wellness. A project of the Rotary Club of Santa Monica and Center for Healthy Aging. Available online. Large Web site discussing diagnoses of dementias, treatment planning, and other mental health illnesses.

Neuroscience Resources for Kids
http//:staff.washington.edu/chudler/aging.html
Neuroscience Resources for Kids has information about the field of neuroscience for children approximately ages 10-18. An individual can also subscribe to a monthly e-mail newsletter with interesting new Web sites and other information about the brain.

Ampalex is a registered trademark of Cortex Pharmaceuticals, Inc.; Aricept is a registered trademark of Eisai Co., Ltd.; BuSpar is a registered trademark of Bristol Myers Squibb; Cognex is a registered trademark of First Horizon Pharmaceuticals; Depakote is a registered trademark of Abbott Laboratories; Exelon is a registered trademark of Novartis Pharmaceuticals Corporation; Lexapro is a registered trademark of Forest Pharmaceuticals; Namenda is a registered trademark of Forest Pharmaceuticals; Paxil is a registered trademark of GlaxoSmithKline; Prozac is a registered trademark of Eli Lilly and Company; Reminyl is a registered trademark of Janssen Pharmaceutica; Risperdal is a registered trademark of Janssen Pharmaceutica; Seroquel is a registered trademark of AstraZeneca; Tegretol is a registered trademark of Novartis Pharmaceuticals Corporation; Xanax is a trademark of Pfizer Inc.; Zoloft is a registered trademark of Pfizer Inc.; Zyprexa is a registered trademark of Eli Lilly and Company.

MKC-231 is under development by Mitsubishi Pharma Corporation, patent pending.

INDEX

MKC-231, 95–96
MMSE. *See* Mini-Mental State Examination
mood, 25, 35, 54, 57
movement disorders
   in Alzheimer's disease, 57
   dementias related to, 12, 29, 69–73
   in frontotemporal dementia, 68
   in Huntington's disease, 71
   in normal aging, 44
   in normal pressure hydrocephalus, 38
   in Parkinson's dementia, 69–70
   in Wilson's disease, 72–73
MRI. *See* magnetic resonance imaging
multi-infarct dementia, 64. *See also* vascular
   dementia
multiple sclerosis, 12–13
muscle atrophy, 44
myelin sheaths, 13, 29

National Institute of Aging (NIA), 14, 44, 96
neoplasias, 43
nerve cells. *See* neurons
nerve growth factors, 94–95
neurodegenerative dementia, 46–47
neurofibrillary tangles
   in Alzheimer's disease, 17–19, 48, 51, 53,
     56–57, 82
   in Lewy body dementia, 67
   in normal aging, 45
   in Parkinson's dementia, 70–71
neurological problems, 4–5
neurons, vi
   in Alzheimer's disease, 46–51
   in dementia, 3–4, 29–33
   in demyelinating diseases, 13
   in frontotemporal dementia, 69
   nerve growth factors and, 94–95
   in Parkinson's disease, 69–70
   structure of, 29–33, 51
neuropathology, 18
neuroscience, vii
neurotransmitters. *See also specific types*
   functions of, 29–32
   in Parkinson's dementia, 69–70
   treatment with, 86–87
NIA. *See* National Institute of Aging
Nissl, Franz, 18

nonsteroidal anti-inflammatory drugs
   (NSAIDs), 60, 84, 93
normal pressure hydrocephalus (NPH), 23, 38
NSAIDs. *See* nonsteroidal anti-inflammatory
   drugs
Nun Study, 96–98

occipital lobe, 34
occupational functioning, 28
older people
   growing population of, 6
   normal aging in, *vs.* dementia, 41–45
   Sundowners syndrome in, 37–38
oxidative stress, 81
oxygen free radicals, 81, 94

paranoid delusions, 54–55, 88
parietal lobe, 34, 49
Parkinson's dementia, 12, 69–71
   vs. Alzheimer's disease, 70–71, 85–86
   causes of, 70, 85–86
   vs. Lewy body dementia, 66
   symptoms of, 29, 69–71
penicillamine, 73
peripheral nervous system, 86–87
personality changes
   in Alzheimer's disease, 25, 54–55
   in frontotemporal dementia, 68
   in Huntington's disease, 71
PET. *See* positron emission tomography
physical examination, 22–23, 47
physical symptoms
   of Alzheimer's disease, 29, 57–58
   of dementia, 29–35
   of Parkinson's dementia, 29, 69–70
plaques. *See* amyloid plaques
pneumonia, 58, 72
positron emission tomography (PET) scans,
   30–31
presenile dementia, 17
presenilin-1, 58, 79
presenilin-2, 58, 79
primitive reflexes, 57–58
prions, 74
progressive diseases, 46–47, 52
proteins. *See specific proteins*
pseudodementia, 38–39

psychiatry, vii
psychology, vii
psychotherapy, 87
psychotic symptoms, 55, 88

Reagan, Nancy, 10
Reagan, Ronald, 10
reflexes, 57–58
Religious Orders Study, 96–98
repair, of neurons, 48
Russia, 11

schizophrenia, 38
secretases, 48–49, 78
sedatives, 76
seizures, 37
selective serotonin reuptake inhibitors (SSRIs), 67, 87–88
selegiline, 94
sensory impairment, 44
silent strokes, 64
snout reflex, 57–58
social functioning, 28, 100
SSRIs. *See* selective serotonin reuptake inhibitors
statins, 60, 93–94
stress, 100
strokes
    causes of, 61–63, 85
    prevention of, 65–66, 85
    transient ischemic attacks and, 64–65
    vascular dementia and, 11, 61–64, 85
subdural hematoma, 41
substance-induced persistent dementia, 75–76
suicide, 72
sulci, 44
Sundowners syndrome, 37–38
swallowing, 56, 57, 58
Swift, Jonathan, 14–15
synapses, vi, 29–32, 59

tangles. *See* neurofibrillary tangles
taste, loss of, 44
tauopathies, 82
tau protein, 51, 69, 82
TBI. *See* traumatic brain injury

temporal lobe, 34, 49, 67, 69, 74
thalamus, 34–35
thiamine, 76
thyroid hormone, 23
TIAs. *See* transient ischemic attacks
transgenic mice, 91
transient ischemic attacks (TIAs), 64–65
trauma, and Huntington's disease, 72. *See also* head trauma
traumatic brain injury (TBI), 60
tremor. *See* movement disorders
twin studies, 79

urinary incontinence, 38
urine tests, 23

vaccines, 91–93
vacuolisation, 69
vascular dementia (VaD), 11, 61–66
    vs. Alzheimer's disease, 64
    causes of, 11, 61–63, 85
    diagnosis of, 64
    prevalence of, 11, 61
    symptoms of, 29, 63–64
    treatment of, 66, 85
ventricles, 44, 53
violence, 55
viral infections, 73–74
vision problems, 44
vitamin B_1, 76
vitamin deficiencies, 23, 76
vitamin E, 81, 94

walking
    in Alzheimer's disease, 57
    in Huntington's disease, 71
    in normal aging, 44
    in normal pressure hydrocephalus, 38
warfarin, 85
Wernicke-Korsakoff syndrome, 76
white populations, 9
Wilson's disease, 12, 13, 72–73

younger people
    dementia in, 12–13
    Huntington's disease in, 72

117

AUTHOR

Dr. Sonja M. Lillrank, M.D., Ph.D., is a Clinical Assistant Professor of Psychiatry and Behavioral Sciences at the George Washington University in Washington DC and is a board certified general adult psychiatrist. She is in private practice and is closely involved in the teaching of psychiatry to medical students as the Clerkship Director for medical students at INOVA Fairfax Hospital Department of Psychiatry in Northern Virginia. Dr. Lillrank received her M.D. degree from University of Tampere, Finland, where she obtained her Ph.D. in neuroscience based on research also conducted at the Karolinska Institut, Department of Pharmacology, in Stockholm, Sweden. She then continued her research as a Fellow and Associate at the National Institutes of Health, National Institute of Mental Health, Clinical Brain Disorders Branch at St. Elizabeth's Hospital in Washington DC. Her published research focuses on modeling neurochemical and neurodevelopmental changes in the brain in psychotic illnesses such as schizophrenia. She did her internship at Johns Hopkins University in Baltimore and residency in psychiatry at the George Washington University in Washington DC.